Mastering 3D Printing in the Classroom, Library, and Lab

Joan Horvath
Rich Cameron

Apress®

Mastering 3D Printing in the Classroom, Library, and Lab

Joan Horvath
Nonscriptum LLC, Pasadena, CA, USA

Rich Cameron
Nonscriptum LLC, Pasadena, CA, USA

ISBN-13 (pbk): 978-1-4842-3500-3
https://doi.org/10.1007/978-1-4842-3501-0

ISBN-13 (electronic): 978-1-4842-3501-0

Library of Congress Control Number: 2018960932

Managing Director, Apress Media LLC: Welmoed Spahr
Acquisitions Editor: Natalie Pao
Copy Editor: Corbin Collins
Coordinating Editor: Jessica Vakili

Cover designed by eStudioCalamar

Distributed to the book trade worldwide by Springer Science+Business Media New York, 233 Spring Street, 6th Floor, New York, NY 10013. Phone 1-800-SPRINGER, fax (201) 348-4505, e-mail orders-ny@springer-sbm.com, or visit www.springeronline.com. Apress Media, LLC is a California LLC and the sole member (owner) is Springer Science + Business Media Finance Inc (SSBM Finance Inc). SSBM Finance Inc is a **Delaware** corporation.

For information on translations, please e-mail rights@apress.com, or visit www.apress.com/rights-permissions.

Apress titles may be purchased in bulk for academic, corporate, or promotional use. eBook versions and licenses are also available for most titles. For more information, reference our Print and eBook Bulk Sales web page at www.apress.com/bulk-sales.

Printed on acid-free paper

To the open source community, particularly to contributors to the RepRap Project, whose vision made consumer 3D printing a reality

Table of Contents

TABLE OF CONTENTS

About the Authors

Joan Horvath and **Rich Cameron** are the cofounders of Nonscriptum LLC, based in Pasadena, California. Nonscriptum consults for educational and scientific users in the areas of 3D printing and maker technologies. Joan and Rich find ways to use maker tech to teach science and math in a hands-on way, and want to make scientific research cheaper and more accessible to the public.

This book is their seventh collaboration for Apress. They teach online classes in 3D printing and maker tech for LERN Network's U Got Class continuing education program. They have also authored online courses for LinkedInLearning/Lynda.com. Links for all of the above are on their website, www.nonscriptum.com.

In addition to her work with Rich, Joan also has an appointment as adjunct faculty for National University's College of Letters and Sciences. She has taught at the university level in a variety of institutions, both in Southern California and online. Before she and Rich started Nonscriptum, she held a variety of entrepreneurial positions, including VP of business development at a Kickstarter-funded 3D-printer company.

ABOUT THE AUTHORS

Joan started her career with 16 years at the NASA/Caltech Jet Propulsion Laboratory, where she worked in programs including the technology transfer office, the Magellan spacecraft to Venus, and the TOPEX/Poseidon oceanography spacecraft. She holds an undergraduate degree from MIT in aeronautics and astronautics and a master's degree in engineering from UCLA.

Rich (known online as "Whosawhatsis") is an experienced open source developer who has been a key member of the RepRap 3D-printer development community for many years. His designs include the original spring/lever extruder mechanism used on many 3D printers, the RepRap Wallace, and the Deezmaker Bukito portable 3D printer. By building and modifying several of the early open source 3D printers to wrestle unprecedented performance out of them, he has become an expert at maximizing the print quality of filament-based printers. When he's not busy making every aspect of his own 3D printers better, from slicing software to firmware and hardware, he likes to share that knowledge and experience online so that he can help make everyone else's printers better too.

Acknowledgments

The consumer 3D-printing ecosystem would not exist in its current form without the open source 3D-printing hardware and software community. The maker community as a whole has also been very supportive. We appreciate how much we learn by looking at projects made by everyone at maker events large and small.

The Apress production team was there for us to solve problems as they arose and let us have great creative freedom otherwise. We dealt most directly with Natalie Pao, Jessica Vakili, Corbin Collins, and Welmoed Spahr, but we also appreciate the many we did not see. This book includes some materials from our other Apress 3D-printing titles, notably the 2014 *Mastering 3D Printing* and the 2016 and 2017 *3D Printed Science Projects* books.

We talked to many 3D-printing professionals and maker-educators to develop this book and we are grateful for the advice, images, and in some cases permission to use screenshots or photographs of their work, which is credited in more detail in the text. On the 3D-printing side of the family, we want to particularly call out Steve Wygant of SeeMeCNC; Shelley Sun and Russell Singer of MAKEiT, Inc.; Mara Hitner and Dave Gaylord at MatterHackers; Diego Porqueras of Deezmaker; Marius Kintel and the other OpenSCAD developers; the teams at Ultimaker and Formlabs; and Thatcher Chamberlain, Metalnat Hayes, Giovanni Salinas, and David Shorey.

Educators (and their students) who particularly inspired us were Simon Huss, Regina Rubio, Tri Nguyen, Karalyn Ramon, and others at the Windward School; Dori Friedman and Paul Way of Crossroads School; Omeed Shahhosseini and Will Kalman, Granada Hills Charter High

ACKNOWLEDGMENTS

School, and maker-educators John Umekubo, Lucie deLaBruere, and Rodney Batschelet. We were inspired to create 3D-printable educational models for visually impaired students by discussions with people in the community of teachers of the visually impaired, notably Mike Cheverie, Lore Schindler, Yue-Ting Siu, and Jim Allan. We have spoken to quite a few librarians to understand their issues and are particularly grateful to Vivienne Bird, Los Angeles Public Library, and Michael Pierce and his colleagues at the Pasadena Public Library.

Finally, we are grateful to our families for putting up with our endless brainstorming and test runs of explanations, particularly Joan's husband Stephen Unwin, Rich's sister, Rachel Cameron, and Diamond the Wonder Puppy.

Introduction

It has only been four years since the original 2014 *Mastering 3D Printing* went to press. In the intervening years, the field has exploded so much that we are to focusing this book on the needs of the educational and scientific markets. Printers have dropped in price down to a few hundred dollars for a basic model and a few thousand for a fairly sophisticated one. Yet adoption has been remarkably slow in education, and we hope to change that.

This book focuses on consumer-level printers and their applications in the educational and scientific environments. We focus primarily on 3D printers that create objects by melting plastic filament, but also include a little about printers that use liquid resin.

3D printing can be defined pretty simply: creating an object by building it up layer by layer, rather than machining it away the way you would by making something from a block of wood, or by squirting something into a mold as you would for injection-molded plastic parts. Its flexibility and the sheer magic of seeing something built from nothing have captured people's imaginations, and it is clear that surprising applications will continue to pop up for years to come.

This book is intended for several audiences. It is meant to be a self-contained tutorial on consumer 3D printers and the open source software that runs them, particularly for educators who are trying to set up or run a school makerspace or librarians who are trying to figure out what to do about a mandate to buy printers or create a community space.

Although we say the book is for "classroom, library, and lab," a broader audience will find the core information helpful. If you are not an educator and want to focus on the 3D printing per se, Chapters 1–6 apply to anyone's use of consumer-level printers; Chapter 8 gives a lot of information on post-processing prints to make them look good; and Chapter 9 discusses making prints as strong as possible. The examples in the other chapters, although primarily classroom oriented, may inspire you for your projects as well.

This book also is intended to be used as a text for a semester-length class or university extension course series covering 3D printing, its applications, and its place in education. It might be paired with an in-depth class on 3D computer-aided design (CAD) software for students interested in teaching engineering and industrial or product design. Similarly, it might be paired with instruction in one of the sculptural 3D-modeling programs for students developing skills in 3D animation or fine art.

Part I (Chapters 1–3) of the book gives background on the history of 3D printers, talks about how the hardware and software work, discusses available materials, and gives some detail of the 3D-printing workflow.

Part II (Chapters 4–6) reviews how to decide what kind of printer you need to buy, based on what you want to build with it and what materials you think you will want to be able to use. This part also reviews what kinds of facilities different 3D printers require, and the hands-on details of dealing with issues that might arise during a print. Finally, this part reviews options you can use to create 3D-printable model files.

Part III (Chapters 7–12) discusses the classroom use of 3D printing in different subject disciplines, with a particular focus on K–12. We start off with a brief introduction to common issues in classroom 3D printing, and then look at art and theater concerns, considering print post-processing topics like gluing, sanding, and painting, as well as a bit about casting jewlery. We also consider engineering concerns, like making a print strong enough for a functional job. Next, we take up using printers in language arts and social studies, and in the elementary school environment. Finally, we talk about how 3D prints might help special-needs students, particularly the visually impaired.

Finally, in Part IV (Chapters 13 and 14), we discuss university and community uses of 3D printing and how to think about careers in 3D printing in the near and long term. Chapter 13 focuses on research into both applications of 3D printing and technology development for 3D printers per se. Chapter 14 winds up the book with a discussion of the opportunities and challenges for teaching entrepreneurship, and tries to predict where the manufacturing and other applications of the technology are likely to be in the near and longer term.

We also include an appendix, in which we have gathered all the links from the book, plus a few news sources that cover the 3D printing world and some books that might provide other places to explore.

Librarians will likely find Chapters 1–6 and 13–14 the most useful, although the materials in Chapters 7–12 may suggest community projects.

The field is still evolving. As in the 2014 *Mastering 3D Printing,* we have avoided detailed descriptions of software packages. We stick with descriptions that will let you get started but will not be wrong three months after publication. We like to say that 3D printing is about as complex as cooking. In cooking terms, you will find that this book has a bias away from providing recipes to follow exactly and instead leans toward teaching you how to cook using your own judgement for the long haul.

If you are just starting your exploration of the field, welcome. Hopefully this book will be a good guide for you, and you will finish it ready to take on challenges and try to help build this new frontier along with us.

PART I

3D Printing: State of the Art

In Part I (Chapters 1–3) we introduce you to 3D printing and discuss why you may want to use a 3D printer instead of other digital manufacturing tools, like laser cutters or computer numerically controlled (CNC) milling machines. We cover the basics of printer technologies. These days, which materials you want to use and what types of things you want to build will drive your choice of printer, and we detail the issues in Chapter 2. Finally, in Chapter 3 we introduce you to the overall workflow of 3D printing and discuss the details of using "slicing" programs to create 3D-printable files.

CHAPTER 1

Why Use a 3D Printer?

In the last five years, 3D printing has gone from a technology hyped as capable of solving any problem to one of disillusionment as people realized it took more expertise than some advertisements implied. Now machines are getting both easier to use and more powerful, and there is a creative explosion in both printer technology and applications. But we are still not quite at the point of clicking Print without any thought on the user's part.

In this book, we attempt to give you a clear-eyed view of the state of the art in 3D printing: what you can do, what you might be able to do soon, and what you really do not want to do, at least not yet. This chapter focuses on when you want to use a 3D printer, and, perhaps more importantly, when you do not. The most fundamental question is: when do you want to use a 3D printer in the first place?

Subtractive vs. Additive

3D printers create objects one layer at a time. The way they do that—by extruding melted plastic, by sintering materials, by hardening resin with UV light—can vary. But the basic premise is the same: a layer of material is created, controlled by a digital design stored in a computer, followed

J. Horvath and R. Cameron, *Mastering 3D Printing in the Classroom, Library, and Lab*,
https://doi.org/10.1007/978-1-4842-3501-0_1

by another layer, and so on until the object appears, seemingly by magic. The key distinction from most other means of manufacturing is that 3D printing is additive—material is not cut away, but is added to a piece as it is built (Figure 1-1).

Figure 1-1. *A 3D printed part in progress*

Consumer-level 3D printers are very simple robots. We often say that they are, more or less, computerized hot glue guns (using a somewhat different plastic, though).

3D printing is a form of *additive manufacturing*, which starts with nothing and builds up parts by laying up material on some sort of build platform. A lot of conventional manufacturing is *subtractive*, meaning that you start with a block of material (like metal or wood) and start cutting away material until you have the part you want plus a pile of sawdust or metal shavings.

3D printers require that you have a 3D computer model of your object in an appropriate format. A photo or other 2D image is not enough—you need to have data that is stored as a full 3D model of the object. We talk about this in depth in Chapter 6. (Although Tinkercad and other software discussed in Chapter 6 can "extrude" an image to make a "2.5D" raised version of a drawing.)

Nature's 3D Printers

3D printing seems like an advanced technology, but many organisms and natural processes have been doing the equivalent for eons. Many rock formations in the southwestern United States were laid down when ancient oceans built up layers of silt. The resulting sandstone has since been carved away by wind, rain, and plant roots. Figure 1-2, taken in Zion National Park in Utah, is an example of the current state of processes that build up material a layer at a time and then erode some of it away. This is a mix of an additive process (like 3D printing), followed by a subtractive process (like conventional manufacturing).

Figure 1-2. *Sandstone layering (Zion National Park, Utah)*

When people watch a natural process, they are often inspired to create a fabrication process that will work the same way. Some types of additive manufacturing have been around for a long time. A very simple example is the humble brick wall. A brick wall is built up one brick at a time, with the addition of a bit of mortar, based on either a formal plan drawn out by an architect or engineer, or perhaps just built out of a contractor's head if the job is routine enough. All the steps you will see in 3D printing are there in building a brick wall: designing a desired end product, planning out how to arrange the layers so that the structure will not fall down while it is being built, and then executing the product one layer at a time. 3D printers add the elements of robotic control to this process of building an object up a layer at a time.

History of Robotic 3D Printing

Charles W. (Chuck) Hull is generally credited with developing the first working robotic 3D printer in 1984, which was commercialized by 3D Systems in 1989. These machines were systems that used a laser to harden liquid resin, and many machines still use this technology. Other early work was taking place at the Massachusetts Institute of Technology (MIT) and the University of Texas.

Meanwhile, S. Scott Crump and Lisa Crump patented fused deposition modeling (FDM) in 1989 and cofounded printer manufacturer Stratasys, Ltd. This technology (more generically called FFF, for *fused filament fabrication*) feeds a plastic filament into a heated extruder and then precisely lays down the material. When key patents expired in 2005, this technology became the basis of the RepRap movement. This book mostly focuses on this type of printer, but we go on some forays into resin stereolithography (SLA) printers as well.

A flurry of patents followed in the early 1990s for various powder-based systems. These systems use inkjets to deposit a binder very precisely on the surface of a bed of powder to create layers on a downward-moving platform. By adding ink to these binders, this process can make full-color prints.

These inkjet 3D-printing patents became the basis for Z Corp, another early printer company that created large industrial printers. Z Corp is now part of 3D Systems. Other powder-based printing technologies manufactured by 3D Systems and others use a laser to fuse powdered plastic or metal together in a process called *selective laser sintering* (SLS).

The RepRap Movement

When some of the key patents expired on the FFF printing method, it occurred to Adrian Bowyer, a senior lecturer in mechanical engineering at the University of Bath in the United Kingdom, that it might be possible to build a filament-extruding 3D printer that could create the parts for more 3D printers (except for readily available electronic and hardware-store components).

Furthermore, Bowyer decided he would put the designs for the parts for his 3D printer out on the Internet, making them available to anyone and encouraging others to improve them—with the requirement that anyone who improved it had to post their versions with the same terms (called an *open source* license). He called this concept the *RepRap* project and obtained some initial funding from the UK's Engineering and Physical Sciences Research Council.

Bowyer's team called their first printer *Darwin* (released in March 2007) and the next one, *Mendel* (released in 2009—for more details, see http://en.wikipedia.org/wiki/RepRap_Project). The printers were named after famous evolutionary biologists because they wanted people to replicate the printers and evolve them as they did so. Files to make the plastic parts were posted online, freely available with alterations and improvements encouraged. Necessary metal parts were ideally available at hardware stores or could be made in a garage. More exotic metal parts, like gears to grip filament and nozzles to push it through, became available for online purchase pretty early on from entrepreneurial printer builders with access to machine tools to make them. Stepper motors and some of the electronic components needed to drive them were already available

online, but became much cheaper and easier to find as the 3D printer
market increased the demand for them.

The early printers were difficult to put together and to get to print well.
In the Czech Republic in 2010, Josef Prusa released a design now called the
Prusa Mendel. It simplified the original Mendel design, and after that there
was an acceleration in printer designs as people tried out the open source
designs, modified them, and posted their own. Prusa Research is now one
of the larger consumer 3D-printer companies, still based in the Czech
Republic. You can look at a "family tree" of this period at `http://reprap.`
`org/wiki/RepRap_Family_Tree`.

After a while there was a transition from making files for printer parts
downloadable to making whole printer kits available for purchase. One
of the better-known kits was the *Makerbot Cupcake CNC*, which started
shipping in April 2009. It was superseded by the *Makerbot Thing-O-Matic*
in 2010. These were mostly made of lasercut wooden parts with some
3D-printed parts (plus of course motors and electronics). Eventually,
Makerbot became one of the earlier commercial consumer printer
companies, and was purchased by Stratasys in 2013.

Crowdfunding and Makers

What really caused a blossoming of different designs, though, was the
availability of funding for hardware projects through *crowdfunding*—
websites that allow entrepreneurs to put out early-stage products and take
contributions from the public to fund development and early production.
Because the key patents had run out, entrepreneurs typically did not
have any type of proprietary technology, which made traditional startup
funding difficult to obtain.

By 2009, 3D-printer developers split into two main camps: those
supplying large, industrial printers (typically with some proprietary
technology) and a big informal network of people working on open source
RepRap or similar filament-based consumer printers.

On April 28, 2009, the *Kickstarter* crowdfunding platform launched (www.kickstarter.com). Kickstarter is one of many *crowdfunding* platforms that allow an entrepreneur to post a project and ask people to support the endeavor. Various crowdfunding platforms have different rules about which types of projects are acceptable, and open source 3D printers are a very good fit for crowdfunding because most crowdfunding sites require a clearly defined project. Developing a 3D printer is a project with a natural endpoint, and often the developer seeking funding offers a printer as the reward for those who support the development.

In 2012, the *Form 1* stereolithography printer raised nearly three million dollars on Kickstarter. Many other 3D printers have raised in the six figures on Kickstarter and other platforms.

Figure 1-3 shows two RepRap heritage printers. Rich designed the 2011 RepRap Wallace (a proof-of-concept machine, never sold commercially) and was a key team member in the design of the 2013 Deezmaker Bukito, which was launched on Kickstarter.

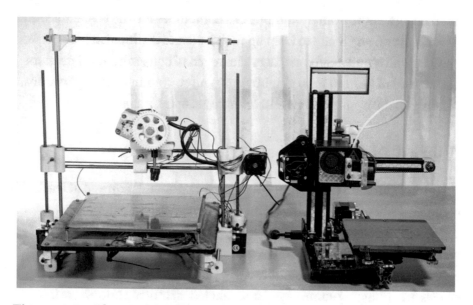

Figure 1-3. *The 2011 Wallace and 2013 Bukito*

At the same time that open source hardware was becoming common, open source or free software also began to stabilize and become useful to a non-expert consumer. Software to design models of 3D printers and to prepare them for printing made great strides around this time. Today, some printers come with proprietary software, but printers that support generic protocols can use free or open source software end-to-end to create models and print them.

It is quite stunning to look at Figure 1-3 and see how rapidly open source printer design matured in a little over two years. Of course, innovation does not stop. In the intervening years, many 3D-printer companies have been started, and many have gone out of business or been acquired. This tumult is typical of a new industry and probably will continue for a while. In Chapters 4 and 5, we talk about how to select a printer for your needs and how to set up a good workflow. For the most part, we have tried to avoid naming brand names because the industry is still changing rapidly.

The pace of development in the field is very rapid; new methodologies are being invented both by commercial companies and by academics, and it can be a real challenge to keep up with it all and distinguish between a new capability and a dubious idea. The reach of consumer-level printers has expanded beyond maker hobbyists to more commercial applications. We discuss the opportunities and limitations in later chapters.

A Word About Kits

Up until about 2013 or so, most consumer 3D printers required at least some assembly. It was worth mentioning in marketing materials if the assembly did not require soldering, since kits in those days often consisted of bags of wires, screws, and small parts. Currently, kits usually require minimal assembly, typically involving tightening a few screws and plugging some keyed and labeled electrical connectors in to the appropriate ports. The cost can be a lot lower than buying a fully assembled printer, since printers often have a few pieces that will fit well in a small package when disassembled, leading to lower shipping costs.

Obviously, though, if you are not comfortable with doing some assembly and calibration, you are likely to be happier with a fully assembled printer. However, even minimal assembly teaches you something about how the machine works, making you more likely to know how to fix something that goes wrong later.

When to Use a 3D Printer

3D printing is a very versatile technology, but there are times when other technologies are preferable. For example, laser cutters and small computer-numerically controlled (CNC) machines may be more appropriate tools in some circumstances. And sometimes you can just use a piece of cardboard and an X-acto knife to make something too.

We can do a comparison of the three common forms of *digital manufacturing*, machines that make something based on a computer file that gives the machine commands resulting in a physical part. Laser cutters work from a 2D file, and 3D printers and CNC machines from different types of 2D and 3D files, although there are similarities. All three have come down in price, although 3D printers probably have made the biggest strides there. The "maker movement," a renewed interest in making physical things, has created a market for these machines, which has bubbled up into professional applications.

For details on 3D printer options, see Chapter 2 for different types of printer. Chapter 4 discusses criteria to use when buying one based on what you want to do. There are a few major drawbacks to a 3D printer in a school environment. First, prints take a long time. A 12-hour or even multi-day print is not uncommon. Second, either you can buy an expensive machine with expensive proprietary raw materials, or you can learn how to use more generic systems with some trial and error. The cost difference can be a factor of 10 or 20, so this is a tricky thing to trade off.

Caution   Be wary of marketing metaphors to paper printers. (We address 3D printer resolution in Chapter 4.) A recent trend we have seen are advertisements for "all in one" 3D printer, scanners, CNC machines, and even laser cutters, sometimes with interchangeable heads. Since the tools have such different requirements to run optimally, we are dubious about this. If your budget is limited, buy just one tool now (we would vote for a 3D printer) and consider branching out in the future.

Laser Cutting vs. 3D Printing

Laser cutters use a laser to burn through material. The bigger the laser, the tougher the material they can cut through. The key word here is *burn*. Because laser cutters are basically vaporizing a thin line of raw material, you have to exercise a lot of care that something unfortunate is not cut. For example, plastics with some chlorine content (like PVC) will emit chlorine gas when cut with a laser cutter. At best, this destroys the machine; at worst, it injures the operator.

Therefore, a laser cutter in a school environment needs very strict protocols to make sure that only things that can be cut safely are ever placed in the machine. A fire extinguisher (along with training on how to use it) is critical too, because sometimes a cut line will catch fire in the machine. Fires are caused by failing to cool the surrounding material and deprive it of the fuel/oxygen mixture required to sustain a fire—for example, by letting the air nozzle get blocked. For that reason, laser cutters need to always have someone watching so that any fire does not get out of hand. Laser cutters need to either be vented to the outside or used with a specialized air filter.

Having said all that, laser cutters are a lot faster than other digital fabrication for anything that is essentially a thick 2D slab. So, if you have pieces that can be slotted together, or if something is a flat cutout (like a stencil), then laser cutters are great. Most consumer-level ones can cut paper, acrylic, and fabric, perhaps leather, and can maybe etch metal, depending on the power of the laser. If you need to make 30 of something in a morning and the geometry and materials fit, a laser cutter might be the way to go, if you can create secure processes for operating it.

Laser cutters are usually between three and ten times the cost of an equivalent-quality 3D printer, but then, they usually have the ability to cut a relatively large part. A tradeoff for many education environments is: a bunch of 3D printers, or one laser cutter? Because of their versatility, we would likely vote for the 3D printer, but your circumstances might warrant a different decision.

CNC Machine vs. 3D Printing

Small CNC machines, like 3D printers, have started to drop in price (and size). Ones that can handle cutting small pieces of wood are available now in desktop-scale sizes. These may have some limited ability to cut soft metals like aluminum, though they need to do so slowly and carefully. Ones designed to cut other metals are still pretty beefy, though, and beyond most hobbyists' expertise level (and budget). Obviously if you want to make things out of a material that a 3D printer cannot make but a small CNC can cut, that can be a discriminator. Typically, in a school environment, a small CNC is used for wood, usually supplementing hand tools.

CNC machines are subtractive, and start with a block of raw material. They make a lot of dust unless they are enclosed very well, and their speed to make one of something is more comparable to a 3D printer than a laser cutter. Like 3D printers, cost rises rapidly with size and range of materials the machine can work with.

Caution   It is usually a bad idea to put a CNC machine, wood-carving machinery, or anything that makes lots of fine dust in the same room as a 3D printer, especially if one or both machines are unenclosed. The dust will get picked up on the filament and clog the nozzle.

Complexity

One of the favorite mantras of 3D printing is *complexity is free*. That is true, to a point. If a part is designed to be 3D printed (as we discuss in the Chapter 6, in particular), then often it does not matter that a shape is complicated. This does matter, a lot, for subtractive technologies because sometimes it is physically impossible to carve certain types of pieces. Subtractive technologies are good if the shape of the final part is not very different from your block, or rod, or sheet of raw material so that not a lot will need to be cut away.

For a 3D printer, the main thing that determines how much time a print will take is how much plastic it contains, including any support material that needs to be printed. There are some exceptions to this, but by and large a simple and complex shape with similar amounts of plastic will take close to the same time to build with a 3D printer. Because a typical 3D print is mostly hollow, the surface area of a model is usually a better predictor of the print time than the volume. The kinetic sculpture in Figure 1-4 (and on this book's cover) is a good example of a complex part that takes a while to print but has no real challenges. It would be very difficult if not impossible to machine.

Size of a print, though, matters a lot. As printers get bigger, their cost rises very quickly. Typical classroom-level printers can build things from a few inches to a foot or so in each dimension. Getting much bigger than that may involve either glue or other assembly techniques to make a large piece out of smaller ones.

Figure 1-4. *A kinetic sculpture by Rich, printed in one piece*

The sculpture in Figure 1-4 is printed in one piece (Figure 1-5) fully assembled. It has matching male and female pivots that let it turn freely. If you want to make one, the open source design is available able at www.youmagine.com/designs/arc-gimbal.

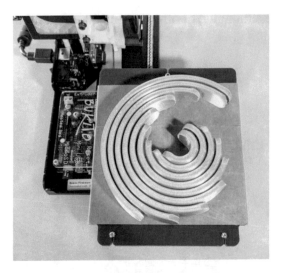

Figure 1-5. *How the piece in Figure 1-4 looks on the printer*

Note   An implication of this ability to make complicated parts is that you may be able to reduce the part count if you go from a traditionally manufactured part to a 3D printed one. The 3D printed part might be able to include a merged version of other parts that might be impossible to mold or machine. This might not come up all that often in a classroom setting, but reducing part count is a valuable thing in industrial applications, where assembly costs money.

Finally, we should not lose sight of the fact that 3D printing feels magical. An industry in-joke is that the second thing you print is a chin rest—so you can stare into your printer as objects seem to materialize from nothing. Even those of us who deal with this every day still sometimes pause to watch and appreciate the power of a technology that can be so inexpensive and yet so capable.

Summary

In this chapter, we laid out the basics of additive manufacturing, building up an object from raw materials one layer at a time, and talked a little about how 3D printers do that. We also gave the highlights of recent history of 3D printer development and showed how the open source RepRap movement turned into an industry. We reviewed the relative merits of the three commonest digital manufacturing machines: 3D printers, laser cutters, and CNC machines. And we discussed the advantage that 3D printers have in creating complex parts, tempered by the fact that 3D prints on affordable 3D printers need to be relatively small.

Moving forward, Chapters 2 through 6 introduce the technology and guide you through selecting the right type of printer and understanding the workflow. Chapters 7 through 14 discuss different applications in the classroom, library, and lab spaces, and give you pointers to many other resources so that you can see what is possible with a consumer-level printer and decide if climbing the learning curve is appropriate for what you would like to do.

CHAPTER 2

3D Printers and Printable Materials

In the last 10 years or so, 3D printers have gone from being large pieces of industrial equipment, to hobbyist novelties, to classroom staples. This chapter reviews the range of technologies that all fall into the broad category of 3D printing. There are many different 3D printers, but fundamentally they all create an object by building up one layer at a time on some sort of platform. As we discuss in Chapter 1, the basic idea of 3D printing (or additive manufacturing, if you prefer) is that you create objects by building them up one layer at a time.

The commonest type of 3D printer works with spools of plastic (called *filament*), which it melts and lays down to create objects. Others use lasers or projectors to harden light-sensitive resin. Still others either sinter powder or lay down binders to form objects from powder. The sheer number of technologies can be overwhelming. There is a lot of experimentation going on in the field at the moment, and hundreds of companies are developing new printers on what seems like a daily basis. The materials available have proliferated too.

In this chapter, we survey the field and give you a basic idea of what each of the technologies is and what it can do. We explain some basic vocabulary so that you can understand what we will be talking about later

J. Horvath and R. Cameron, *Mastering 3D Printing in the Classroom, Library, and Lab*, https://doi.org/10.1007/978-1-4842-3501-0_2

in the book. Later chapters focus more on the how-to aspects: the software of 3D printing (Chapters 3 and 6), things to consider when buying a printer (Chapter 4), and how to fit a printer into your space and daily routines (Chapter 5).

Note   The 3D printing world uses metric measurements, and you will need to get comfortable with them if you are not already. The commonest measures you will encounter are millimeters (mm) and degrees Celsius. If you are used to Imperial units, 25.4 mm is an inch. To convert temperature in degrees Celsius to Fahrenheit, multiply the temperature in Celsius by 9/5, then add 32 degrees. So, an extruder temperature of 210 C is the same as 410 F.

Filament Printers

By far the commonest consumer-level 3D-printing technology is *fused deposition modeling,* sometimes called FDM (which technically applies to just one manufacturer) or more generically FFF for *fused filament fabrication.* In this book, we just refer to these printers as *filament 3D printers.* These printers pull plastic filament off a spool, melt it, and lay down the melted plastic in a fine line, typically around 0.2 mm high and a few times as wide.

Figure 2-1 shows a typical filament printer, which would have a spool of filament next to it if it were running. We have also labeled the common convention for naming the axes of a printer. The *x*-axis here is left to right, the *y*-axis is toward and away from you, and the *z*-axis is vertical.

There are several different architectures of filament printers, which we can divide into *Cartesian* and *non-Cartesian*. Cartesian printers (like the one in Figure 2-1) have one motor or pair of motors for each drive axis. Non-Cartesians have no particular relationship between any one motor and axis.

Figure 2-1. *A typical consumer 3D printer*

The commonest non-Cartesian architecture is the *delta* printer, or *deltabot*, which uses a mechanism similar to those found in many pick-and-place robots. A typical delta is shown in Figure 2-2. Deltas are commonest for applications needing big build areas; Figure 2-3 is a photo of the giant demonstration deltabot, the Part Daddy, made by the same manufacturer as the consumer printer in Figure 2-2.

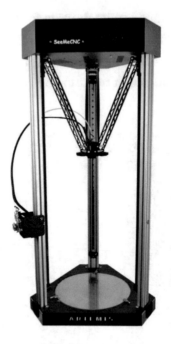

Figure 2-2. *The Artemis deltabot*

Note   There are philosophical debates about whether Cartesians or deltas are "better" for any purpose, somewhat along the lines of debates about the virtues of Windows versus Mac personal computers. In the end, the quality of manufacture and the features you need should drive your choice.

Figure 2-3. *The Part Daddy demonstrator*

Parts of a Filament Printer

A filament printer is pretty simple—a common analogy is to call it a computerized hot glue gun. However, there are several critical parts that affect reliability, print quality, and what kinds of materials you can use.

Stepper Motors

Consumer 3D printers usually have four or more *stepper motors,* commonly called *steppers*. As the name implies, these are precise motors that move their shafts in predefined angular steps. The availability of very reliable, precise, yet cheap steppers like those in Figure 2-4 has been an enabler for many consumer goods. Typically, one motor drives each axis (sometimes two, on the vertical (z-) axis) by being coupled through pulleys to a belt or cable, or to a drive screw for an axis (often used for the z-axis). Another motor drives the extruder gear. The steps per millimeter of your gears (how much an axis, or the filament, moves as the motor turns) is one of the things limiting how accurate a 3D printer can be, although it is not usually the principal limitation. Motors for 3D printers typically have 200 steps per revolution.

Figure 2-4. *A stepper motor*

Control

3D printers are controlled by microcontrollers. Many of these use a processor that is an adaptation or descendant of the Arduino open source microcontroller standard. Surprisingly, many printers run on very little computing horsepower. As of early 2017, most printers use *open-loop control*, meaning that they do not have sensors checking that the printer is running as planned, except for sensors monitoring key temperatures (of the print bed and extruder). Deltas take more processing power than

Cartesians, generally speaking, and you may want a more powerful controller on a delta to keep up.

3D PRINTER CONTROLLERS

The most common type of 3D printer controller is based on the ATmega2560, an 8-bit microcontroller that runs at 16 Mhz. The first 3D printer controller to use this processor was the RAMPS board (short for RepRap Arduino Mega Pololu Shield). This was a shield, or daughterboard, designed to be used with the Arduino Mega development board that was designed to carry several small stepper driver boards in a form factor originally designed by electronics manufacturer Pololu. Most modern versions have the Atmega2560 chip onboard rather than using a separate circuit board, but many are still designed to use replaceable stepper drivers in the Pololu form factor. More advanced stepper drivers are now available in pin-compatible formats that allow you to upgrade your printer or replace a damaged driver.

There are several different projects developing open source firmware to run on these 8-bit microcontrollers. The most common of these is the Marlin firmware. Some newer controllers use 32-bit ARM microcontrollers running at 48–120 Mhz. These are generally designed to use a specific firmware, such as Smoothieware or Duet Firmware, and they are generally not compatible with other firmware options the way 8-bit controllers are.

Most printers do not need to be tethered to a computer. If they are, it is to feed the commands to create a model, not to directly control the motors and temperatures.

A printers runs some sort of firmware on its controller to do that low-level control. *Firmware* is just software that is used to control a machine. Many printers that are descendants of the RepRap project described in Chapter 1 run a variation of the open source Marlin firmware. Makerbots and their distant cousins and clones tend to run a version of the Sailfish firmware.

Build Platform

Prints are created on a flat platform, interchangeably referred to as the print *bed* or print *platform*. It might or might not have a heater, which allows you to use more materials, as we discuss in detail in Chapter 4. Depending on the printer design, the print bed may move in one or two directions, or not at all.

Extruder

The *extruder* is the part of the printer that melts and moves the filament. It is made up of several parts. We have already mentioned the extruder drive gear and its motor, which push the filament into the hot end. The hot end in turn is comprised of a heater, a nozzle, and a sensor (called a *thermistor*) to sense how hot the nozzle is.

The nozzles are very precise. They typically measure 0.35–0.50 mm in diameter and can be made entirely of metal, or they may be lined with a material called PTFE to minimize jamming. All-metal hot ends are required for printing many materials, as discussed in Chapter 5.

The hot end includes a heating element and a sensor to regulate temperature, a thermal transition zone (often with a heatsink and fan on the cold end), and a nozzle that is usually made of brass. Recently hardened-steel and ruby-tipped nozzles have appeared—some filaments are very abrasive, and these are more resistant to abrasion. Figure 2-5 is a close-up of a nozzle.

Figure 2-5. *A nozzle*

How Printing Works

First, filament has to be pulled from the spool into the printer, usually with a gear driven by a stepper motor. There are a variety of geometries for this. Sometimes a gear is right next to where the plastic will be melted (the hot end), and sometimes it is separated by a long tube, called a *Bowden tube.* Extruders with a gear pulling in filament without an intermediary tube are called *direct-drive* extruders (though, confusingly, the same term is used to distinguish extruders with the drive gear mounted directly to the motor from ones that have a gear reduction). In either case, the gear gripping the filament is called the extruder *drive gear.* Figure 2-6 shows the drive gear on a Bowden-style printer.

Some manufacturers like direct-drive extruders; many have moved now to some form of Bowden extruder. The main advantage of having the gear right at the extruder is simplicity, though it also means that the motor is being carried around with the hot end, which may mean slower printing and other issues.

27

Figure 2-6. *Extruder gear on a printer with a Bowden tube*

A print starts with a 3D CAD design, which is turned into a series of commands for the stepper motor and the temperature controls. This process is discussed in detail in Chapters 3 and 6. Once those commands are loaded onto the printer, via cable, SD card, or wireless connection, the printer will first heat up the nozzle and the platform (if it has a heater). Once everything is up to temperature and the printer performs whatever self-checks it is capable of, printing begins.

The first layer of the print has to stick well to the platform. There are various techniques for ensuring this. Some involve software settings (Chapter 3), and others are related to using the correct platform surface for the material you are printing (Chapter 4). Assuming that the print sticks, as a layer builds up there are areas that do and do not have plastic within one layer. This means that the nozzle will be extruding during some parts of the layer, and not during others.

During the time that the printer is not laying down plastic, the extruder gear will first pull the filament back a bit to relieve pressure in the nozzle. This is called *retraction*, and getting it right is something of a black art that involves a process of trial and error for particular combinations of printer hardware and filament material. Poor retraction settings can make a print stringy or blobby, like the one in Figure 2-7.

Figure 2-7. *A print with poor retraction settings*

If the print fails to stick, most printers do not know that and will happily continue to print. This will result in a big pile of plastic (Figure 2-8). It is something of a rite of passage to leave a printer for a while and come back to a big hairball. Take a picture, sigh, and take comfort that you are now an official member of the 3D-printing tribe.

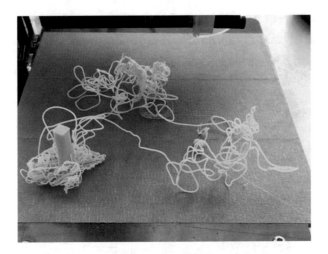

Figure 2-8. *A failed print*

Suppose that you were printing something that had a part sticking out, like someone reaching out an arm. As you built up your print layer by layer, you would eventually reach the first layer of the bottom of the arm. But as you laid out plastic to form the first layer, it would just fall down since there was nothing to support it. To address problems like that, we use support material. *Support* is extra material that is added to the model to allow it to print a layer at a time. Figure 2-9 shows a print with support. The process of creating support is discussed in Chapter 3.

Printers can handle *overhangs* of about 45 degrees— the subsequent layers overlap a bit and allow you to print these moderate slopes. Printers can also *bridge* over open areas. If you are printing a hollow cube, for instance, the top will be over open space, but supported on all four sides. Many of the support and bridging decisions that need to be made are somewhat automated these days, but in Chapter 3 we talk about the human intervention that is still required.

Figure 2-9. *A print with support*

Assuming that everything went well, you will have a print that builds up from the platform layer by layer. The layers will be more visible in some filaments than others. Layer height is something that most printers allow you to set; common heights run from about 0.1 to 0.3 mm. Figure 2-10 is a close-up of the output from the Part Daddy giant printer in Figure 2-3, which is a little easier to see than some. (This printer uses plastic pellets rather than filament, which is why the colors are variable.)

Figure 2-10. *A close-up of layers*

Filament Choices

There are many choices for 3D-printer filament. Your printer, however, will likely only be able to handle a subset of them, and will either use 3 mm or 1.75 mm diameter filament. The quality of your 3D-printing filament will make the difference between endless frustration and a good experience, so let's go over what "filament quality" means first.

Consumers 3D printers, as we have just seen, are really not all that sophisticated. They have, in a way, outsourced their complexity to their filament. Consistency and quality is better now than it was a few years ago, but can still be uneven.

If you are 3D printing, you need a pair of digital calipers to check your filament's diameter. A "3 mm" filament will typically be about 2.85 mm. A 1.75 mm filament will usually be about that. If you have a printer that uses cartridges, you will need to assume that the extra money you pay for your filament is taking care of this step for you. Be sure to adjust the filament diameter setting in your software (Chapter 3) to the actual value of your filament diameter. Typically we just leave the value at 1.75 or 2.85 without adjustment most of the time these days. Figure 2-11 shows checking filament diameter with a pair of calipers.

Figure 2-11. *Checking filament diameter with a pair of calipers*

Tip   If your printer stops extruding mid-print, your first suspect should be a bulge in the filament, which will jam the extruder. The extruder gear will also usually chew into the filament and therefore have a lot of ground filament in it. Brush the ground filament out gently and measure the filament. If it is significantly wider than you expected, break off a few meters and measure again.

The other filament problem that can cause this symptom is filament impurity or poor color mixing. Again, try breaking off some and printing again. If your printer has a restart function, it probably will not work in this case, because you do not know how long the filament has been grinding. You will probably have to restart from the beginning.

There are a lot of different filaments available. We discuss some of the commonest ones, and what 3D-printer hardware and software you need to use them.

Tip   Filaments come labeled with a range of appropriate temperatures for the extruder and the platform (often a disturbingly large range). There may be a label on the spool or on the website where you ordered it. If in doubt, start in the middle of the range. See the discussions of settings in Chapter 3 to see whether you should move up or down if you do not like the results.

Filaments need to be kept in a cool, dry place. Do not open a spool of filament out of its shrink wrap until you are ready to use it, because keeping it sealed will keep moisture out of it. After a while, you will have a bunch of partial spools on the go. We keep ours in airtight plastic boxes— a 5-gallon paint bucket with a good lid works well; Joan is partial to 22-liter stacking plastic boxes with good seals.

Nylon is particularly sensitive to humid conditions. If nylon gets damp, the water will pop and sizzle out as it heats up, leaving pits and gaps in the print. If you live someplace with routinely high humidity, you may want to explore reviews of the various filament-drying systems out there, or DIY equivalents.

Caution   Many low-cost printers have no temperature limiters in their software or hardware and will be perfectly happy trying to heat the nozzle to the point where it will burn, or the heated bed to beyond its design temperature. Check your manufacturer's limitations before trying a filament that your printer was not designed to use.

PLA

By far the commonest filament material is PLA, polylactic acid. It is a biodegradable, corn-based (sometimes sugarcane-based) plastic. It melts at a relatively low temperature and will stick to a variety of platform surfaces. PLA usually requires an extruder temperature of around 210 degrees C.

One of the reasons it is so popular is that PLA does not require a heated platform. Low-cost printers usually suggest that you put blue painter's tape (1.88-inch wide 3M ScotchBlue 2090 works well) and use that as your surface. If you *do* have a heated platform, follow your manufacturer's suggestions for what to put on the bed. Often it will be plain glass, or you might smear on some glue stick first. Do not use blue tape on a heated platform—doing so will create a sticky mess.

The downside of PLA is that, well, it melts at a low temperature. A PLA print on a hot car dashboard will warp and creep. (*Creeping* is a tendency to flow slowly under pressure—for example, a PLA print might develop a dent if something is pressing against it in a warm room.) If that is not an issue, PLA is a very good material for quick prototypes, student projects, and the like.

There are specialty *filled PLA* mixes that contain stone, wood, metal, or glow-in-the-dark fine particles. Objects made with this can look surprisingly like they are made of the respective substance, with a bit of polishing. However, these mixes are hard on nozzles and tend to abrade them; hardened or ruby-tipped nozzles can get around this problem. There are also formulations of PLA that have a nice sheen without any post-processing. Experiment a little (many filament sellers have sample packs) to see what you might like to work with.

Figure 2-12 shows the bad side of PLA: a garden sign that sat out in a California agave desert garden in the sun for about two years gradually sagged under its own weight. Back in Chapter 4, Figure 4-2, on the other hand, shows how fine a finish one can get with PLA.

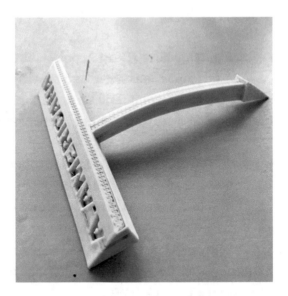

Figure 2-12. *PLA sign after time in the California sun*

PET

PET (polyethylene terephthalate) is a very common plastic in the non-3D-printing world, used for water bottles and many other things. PETG is a type of PET that is often used in 3D printing; some varieties are translucent. You can in principle print PETG on blue tape, although people use heated beds if they have one. It needs an extruder temperature higher than PLA—around 230–260 C. PET filaments are typically a little more expensive than PLA, sometimes as much as twice the price. But they can look really good, particularly if you want something transparent, and they are not as vulnerable to warm temperatures as PLA is.

ABS

Acrylonitrile butadiene styrene (ABS) is the plastic used for LEGO bricks, among many other things. It is durable and far less vulnerable to warping in warm temperatures. The flip side of that is that it requires a high nozzle temperature—from about 220–260 C. A heated bed is also an absolute requirement for ABS, at 90–110 C. People often use PET or Kapton tape on a heated bed for ABS. As ABS cools, it wants to shrink and will pull up from the bed, as you can see in the print that was stopped after a few layers shown in Figure 2-13. Some trial and error is required to get it to stick and lay flat.

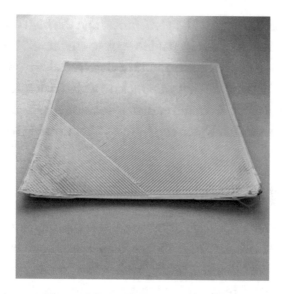

Figure 2-13. *An ABS part that pulled up from the heated bed*

Caution   Although we recommend ventilation with any 3D printer, ABS fumes in particular are an issue. However, blowing a fan directly on the print will tend to make it fail. Arrange your ventilation if possible to be pulling air off the print rather than blowing on it.

ABS can be smoothed and post-processed in a variety of ways. We talk about some of those in Chapter 8, where we discuss art and theater applications.

Nylon

Nylon is a strong printing material, which also requires a high temperature of around 240–270 C. Be sure your nozzle is all-metal before trying to print with nylon, because nozzles lined with plastic cannot handle that high a temperature.

The biggest challenge with nylon, other than the high extruder temperature, is that it does not want to stick to anything. The best option we have found is a cold platform made of Garolite LE, a type of composite. Failing that, we have heard that glue stick on a platform heated to about 75 degrees C will work. As noted earlier, nylon also needs to be kept very dry, or pitting can result. Nylon can be dyed after printing with dyes appropriate for it.

Challenging Filaments

Some materials are difficult to print well. Filaments that are very strong tend to require correspondingly higher temperatures and often want to peel up from the print bed. Some printers can handle materials like polycarbonate, which typically requires higher nozzle and bed temperatures than consumer machines can achieve safely.

There are also filaments that are flexible which can create parts that also can flex. However, they tend to jam in the extruder, particularly for printers using 1.75 mm filament and Bowden tubes.

Dissolvable Support

Some printers have more than one extruder. One reason for buying such a machine is to allow the use of support material that can be dissolved away, either with water or other chemicals.

The commonest water-soluble support, PVA (polyvinyl alcohol), is basically Elmer's Glue. As you might imagine, it has a tendency to clog nozzles, and it has to be extruded fairly cold. Check your local rules about disposal—you should not put water full of dissolved glue into your plumbing. PVA has to be kept extremely dry, for obvious reasons. It also tends not to stick well to the other materials you are using to make your print.

Other materials like HIPS (high impact polystyrene) dissolve in *limonene* (a solvent made from oranges), but this leaves you with a rather smelly mess to deal with.

In other words, this is not a particularly easy route to go. You will need to talk to your local waste-disposal person to see how best to handle your waste stream. In the end, you may decide to stick with support you can pull off with pliers. We talk more about support in Chapter 3's discussion of software settings.

Multimaterials vs. Multiple Extruders

The other reason you might buy a printer with multiple extruders is to print objects in more than one color at a time. With only one extruder, 3D printers print with just one color of filament for the entire print. In essence, you develop two interleaved computer models, one for each color, and the printer alternates extruders in each layer. Because the extruders would interfere if they tried to print at the same time, typically dual-extruder prints take longer than single-extruder ones do because one extruder prints, then wipes itself off (so it does not dribble on the layer once it is done), and so on, back and forth.

Alternatively, some machines now come with a device that can take filament from two spools and splice a mixed filament to mimic what two heads would have done, but with one nozzle. This is an interesting development to watch; there are some aftermarket devices available as add-ons to existing printers.

Aftermarket Upgrades

If you want to be able to print some materials that will not stick to your original print bed material, there are now a variety of aftermarket materials you can stick on to your platform. A commonly used one is BuildTak (`www.buildtak.com`), which can be glued on to your existing platform. The only issue is that some materials stick *too well* to BuildTak, and getting the prints off it is challenging. You will need to recalibrate your printer if you add a clip-on or stick-on platform on top of your original. See "Calibrating Your Printer" in Chapter 5.

Similarly, there are replacement third-party nozzles. Here, however, the replacement process is more sophisticated, and if you are not a tinkerer who is comfortable with building a printer from a kit, you probably should not go that route.

Advanced Filament Printers

As the consumer and higher-end "prosumer" markets expand, some specialty printers have emerged. Some are very large, having a build volume of a cubic meter or more. Some have up to five extruders, or one of the multimaterial extruders we mentioned earlier.

Another niche is occupied by Markforged (`www.markforged.com`). This company has a printer that lays down nylon in parallel with another head that lays down one of several continuous fibers. Thus, they are 3D printing carbon fiber or other composite parts; Markforged has stated in webinars that its early adopters often use their printers to make tooling. Some Markforged printers use a filament with chopped carbon fiber filler, which increases the stiffness of the base nylon. This evolution of materials with custom printers is probably a niche that will grow as specialty applications emerge; novel materials are now driving a lot of the 3D-printing universe as the printers become more commoditized.

Markforged is also one of several companies developing printers that are designed to print with filament (or, in some cases, rods) with a high percentage of metal filler. Metal-filled filament is available for many printers, but although most of these filaments can only give the appearance of metal, these machines are designed to create real metal parts by allowing you to put the printed parts into a furnace that will burn out the plastic matrix material and fuse the metal particles together.

3D-PRINTING PENS

3D-printing "pens" (Figure 2-14) heat up 3D-printing filament (usually 1.75 mm) and allow you to freehand draw with the melted plastic. They are useful for gluing together broken prints, since you can use a thin line of the same material as you are using for your 3D print. In other words, they are more or less hot glue guns that use 3D printer filament.

The pens can also be used to do 3D freehand drawing. However, unless you have really steady hands, it is not as easy as it looks. Cover a piece of cardboard with the same blue painter's tape you would use on a cold 3D-printer platform and use it as your work area.

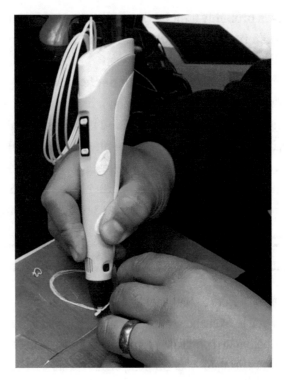

Figure 2-14. *A 3D printing pen*

Vendors sell short strips of PLA filament to use with these devices, but you can use 1.75 mm regular 3D-printer filament, which is much cheaper. We usually cut a few meters or so off at a time to use because the regular spools can be annoying to use with a pen. You can use as many colors as you want in one design, since you will just load strips of filament one at a time to create an object. We usually save the last few meters of filament on a spool to use with pens.

Some pens can use both PLA and ABS, with an ability to set temperatures appropriate for both, and most have a speed control to manage how much plastic you are using at a time. Using one of these pens can be a good exercise in building your intuition about what a 3D printer is doing, as you will most likely make a stringy mess the first time you use a pen.

Concerns about ventilating an area where you are melting plastic, ABS in particular, still apply with a pen. And of course the pen tip gets very hot, just like the extruder on a 3D printer. If you are using PLA, you will need to have some sort of air flow anyway to cool the material as it hardens out of the pen if you want to build in 3D.

There are stencils and such things too; search online for "3D art pen" for examples and videos. Eiffel Tower models are the aspirational thing to build, but you obviously should not start there. No computer modeling is required to use a 3D pen, but manual dexterity and a bit of artistic ability help. Pens with good temperature control and ability to use multiple materials cost about $50–$100.

Resin Printers: SLA and DLP

The consumer resin printer market has been coming into its own recently with a great deal of experimentation. There are two types of resin printer on the market right now: stereolithography (SLA) and Digital Light Processing (DLP). Technically, both are SLA, but the terminology is used somewhat ambiguously. Laser SLA printers use optics to move around an ultraviolet laser spot to cure UV-curable resin within one layer at a time. This layer is peeled off the bottom of a tank (or dropped down into the tank, in the older but now less-common top-down orientation), and then the next layer is cured, and so on. Figure 2-15 shows a Formlabs Form 2, one of the higher-end consumer SLA machines.

DLP, on the other hand, uses a projector to cure a whole layer at a time. A new class of DLP printers uses a cell phone screen as the projector. In Chapter 4's discussion of purchase decisions for these printers, we go into the pluses and minuses of these in more detail, and the operational issues.

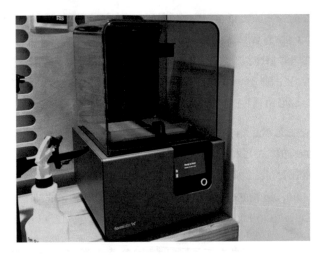

Figure 2-15. *A Formlabs Form 2 SLA resin printer*

Printing Process

Resin 3D printers have an ability to create far finer detail than filament-based printers. A resin printer is limited by its laser spot size (SLA) or the pixel size of the projector (DLP). This means that resin prints can have very smooth surfaces relative to those created by a printer using filament.

Resin printers still need to create support, but the nature of the support is a little different. Typical printers are "bottom-up" and build a layer at a time, which is peeled off the bottom of a tray. To survive the peeling process with every layer, support is required. However, the object prints upside-down and support is primarily withstands the forces associated with peeling off the bottom at the end of each layer. Figure 2-16 shows a print building upside-down on a Form 2. The greenish glow is the laser.

Printers that use a laser to cure resin use a series of coordinates that the laser spot moves through, philosophically similar to the commands that control a filament-based printer. They can generally move the laser spot much faster than a printer can move a heated nozzle, though. Although most have proprietary software, some of them have adapted software developed for filament printing.

Printers that use a projector need a series of 2D images, one for each layer. Some of these printers have an HDMI port as an input, and their software treats the printer as a second monitor on which it displays those images. A popular way to run these machines is to connect a Raspberry Pi running NanoDLP to avoid tying up a larger computer. This avoids potentially ruining a print or even damaging the printer if the computer tries to display something else on that "screen."

Figure 2-16. *A resin print in progress*

Post-processing

Post-processing is required on SLA prints, and typically involves washing off the print with isopropyl alcohol to remove uncured resin and exposing the print to UV light to ensure that the resin is fully cured. This can be a challenge in environments that are not set up for disposing of chemicals.

Each manufacturer will have a process for its own resins; read the process on the manufacturer's site before purchasing your printer so you are sure you will be set up to handle it. Typically, prints emerge from the printer a little sticky and need to be washed off and light-cured. Figure 2-17 shows a resin print just after its wash but before curing. You can also see how much more open support is on a resin printer.

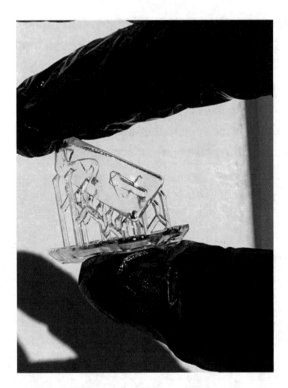

Figure 2-17. *Washing off a resin print*

Notice that this process requires wearing nitrile gloves to keep the resin off your skin. We talk a little more about resin printers in Chapter 5.

Materials

Resin printers use a variety of light-cured resins. Most of them are sensitive to UV light so that you do not have to use them in a dark room, since visible light does not harden them. But because by definition you cannot see UV light, you might be surprised if you don't control the environment around the printer. For example, having a resin printer in direct sunlight can destroy the printer (or at least its resin tank) by hardening a brick of resin into it.

Much of the development in resin 3D printing at the moment is in proprietary resins with special properties. Formlabs, for example, has a high-temperature resin that it says can be used for injection molds. Biocompatible resins for dental work has been an active area of study as well. Because the materials are so crucial, many manufacturers have closed systems with materials cartridges and proprietary software. These may have great properties, but they will be correspondingly expensive.

Some specialty resin applications include the following:

- High-temperature for injection molds

- Biocompatible resins for dental work

- Castable resins for jewelry

- Resins that cure into a flexible material

Formlabs (`www.formlabs.com`) has been an innovator in the materials space. If you want to know more, you can read up on its proprietary materials on the website, which includes case studies.

Other Technologies

The overall field of 3D printing has been expanding in many different directions. There are a few other major categories of printer that are unlikely to come into the classroom in the near term, but given the rate of progress, one never knows!

There are some just-for-fun technologies, like a printer that makes pancakes (`www.pancakebot.com`) and ones that print in sugar or other foodstuffs. But the industrial market has been moving onward too. In this section, we talk about some of the categories of industrially oriented printers.

SLS

One of the oldest technologies in this space is selective laser sintering (SLS). Typically, a very fine powder is spread on a build platform, and a laser is used to sinter the powder together. More and more powder is added as the print grows. SLS can be used to make very fine, detailed prints. SLS prints do not need support, because the unfused powder acts as a support. However, the powder is very fine and hard to deal with, and SLS has been an expensive technology. Some "desktop" SLS machines are beginning to come on the market, and this may be an area to watch.

Many machines that print metal use a process called direct metal laser sintering (DMLS), which is the SLS process used for metals. Metal powder has to be worked in an inert atmosphere to prevent fires, so DMLS machines are very expensive since they need to be completely enclosed and filled with an inert gas. Other processes like selective laser melting (SLM) and electron beam melting (EBM) use even higher power to more fully fuse metal powder.

The alternative discussed earlier in this chapter under "Advanced Filament Printers" is to mix the powder with something else. This too is an evolving area to watch.

Binder Jetting and Material Jetting

There are also processes that use a powder bed which do not require a laser (or other highly-directed heat source). These processes typically use an inkjet head similar to what you would find in a desktop photo printer. Instead of heating the powder to fuse it, they deposit glue or other binding agents onto the powder. Binder-jetting machines typically use gypsum powder, and can deposit ink along with the binding agent to create full-color prints. Binder jetting can also be done with metal, but that requires a second step in which the loosely bound particles are infused with a lower-temperature metal. Some machines even sinter nylon powder by using inkjet heads to deposit sensitizing and/or inhibiting agents to the powder before heating it with a more diffuse heat source.

Other processes do away with the powder entirely and use inkjet heads to deposit liquid resin. These printers deposit tiny droplets of UV-sensitive resin and then quickly expose it to UV light to solidify it. This process requires that multiple materials be used—a build and support material at least—and can be used to produce prints with gradients of color and even of material properties like flexibility.

Bioprinting

Printing with biological materials has become fairly mainstream now in lab environments. In some cases, the printer is using some sort of paste to create an object for a biology lab. In others, the printer is very precisely squirting a liquid. The lower-cost "bioprinters" are basically a robotic pipette that can move in three dimensions; there are several competitors in this space already, and there will probably be more. Search for "bioprinter" to see the huge range of capabilities and price ranges.

Organovo (`www.organovo.com`) has been printing human tissue, as have other researchers. Right now most people are looking at projects like skin or ear repairs, but there is long-term interest in building entire human organs. At the other end of the scale are companies like SE3D (`www.se3d. com`), which makes simple syringe-based devices that come with kits of materials to use with the printer to learn biological concepts.

Summary

This chapter reviewed the different types of 3D-printer technology available in the consumer market, with a particular focus on printers that use plastic filament. We also gave a brief introduction to other technologies, particularly printers that use liquid resin. 3D-printer evolution is being driven now by inventions of new materials, too, and we discussed some of the wide variety of materials you might want to explore.

CHAPTER 3

3D Printer Workflow and Software

People are often startled and intimidated when they discover that a 3D printer is not really the same as a paper printer. Although some consumer 3D printers have a "print" button, there are some steps needed to get to the point of pushing it, not to mention the need to monitor what happens afterwards. We prefer to think of 3D printing as more like cooking than printing. Just as you would not expect to cook by just pressing a "bake" button without setting some temperatures and timers first, 3D printing requires some knowledge of your printer, the materials you are using, and the design you are trying to print. If any of those have issues, getting good results is challenging.

As happens with cooking, everyone wants to start out creating a multitier wedding cake. However, it is wise to try for brownies instead, at least for a while. In this chapter, we help you understand what is hard to print versus what is easy, and give you some insight into more sophisticated techniques. Different printers have evolved variations on the basic workflow. Some are the equivalent of an Easy-Bake Oven, whereas others are like equipment in a commercial kitchen, for similar reasons of capability versus complexity. Your expectations need to match your hardware. Price is not always a guide to capability and quality in the current market; see Chapter 4's discussion on how to buy a printer.

J. Horvath and R. Cameron, *Mastering 3D Printing in the Classroom, Library, and Lab*, https://doi.org/10.1007/978-1-4842-3501-0_3

As you will see, unlike with cooking, some basic computer skills are necessary to get started. This chapter walks through the steps needed to go from zero to plastic in as generic a way as possible, with some nods to common variations on the theme. 3D-printing software is updated often, so the precise options we show here may change by the time you read this. The overall workflow should stay much the same, though. For that reason, we have just a few screenshots and narrate the types of printer settings rather than go step-by-step through any particular program.

Workflow Overview

3D printing typically requires three steps (Figure 3-1) that might be combined into fewer than three pieces of software, might require some scrolling around on a screen on your printer for the last step, or might involve other variations. In all cases, though, you need to create or acquire a 3D *computer-aided design* (CAD) model, slice this model into layers and generate the commands needed to physically create the model, and, finally, physically create the print.

This chapter is mostly focused on the middle step of slicing the model and creating commands. Some printers use proprietary software that integrates the last two steps. They may automate some of the decisions we describe in this chapter, or have hard-coded some compromise settings that will work decently in some common situations but perhaps create bad prints in others. As the market has expanded, printers have fallen into two camps: printers with proprietary ecosystems (typically more expensive) and *open* printers that allow you to use a variety of free software and generic materials. The *closed* printers position themselves as easier to use, and the open ones as allowing users more flexibility.

Figure 3-1. *3D-printing workflow*

Note   For historical reasons, people sometimes refer to the set of software that runs an automated tool like a 3D printer as its *toolchain*. The word does not imply any physical objects—in the case of a 3D printer, at least. We use the word *workflow* here, which we feel may be more familiar in educational or scientific settings.

Models

The first step in the 3D-printing process is developing a 3D model of the design you want to create. This is done in CAD software, which we introduce here and explore in depth in Chapter 6.

Types of 3D-Printable Files

Typical consumer 3D printers want a model to be in stereolithography (STL) format. This format is quite old and inefficient, but universal. When software generates an STL file, it converts the surface to a mesh of triangles. An STL file consists of a giant list of the coordinates of the three vertices of each triangle in 3D space, and the orientation of the normal vector to the plane of that triangle.

A similar standard supported by many slicers is an OBJ file, an open format originally developed by Wavefront Technologies that also supports texture mapping for color and NURBS curvature, though use of these features is rare and they are ignored by slicers if present. A superset standard that can be a grouping of multiple STL files is an additive manufacturing (AMF) file, which also supports material definitions required for printing with multiple filaments (for different colors or different material properties). More recently, Microsoft has formed a consortium to introduce the 3D manufacturing (3MF) format, which has similar capabilities (for more, see `https://3mf.io/what-is-3mf/`).

File Repositories

The other way to get an STL file is to download one that someone else has already created. Many repositories are full of files that people have put out for free, including `www.thingiverse.com`, `www.youmagine.com`, `www.instructables.com`, and `www.pinshape.com`. There are repositories on `www.github.org` that include 3D-printable models as well.

For better or worse, these repositories are populated by anyone who wants to post something. Although many of the designs are amazing, some of the objects may never have actually been printed, or the designer might be nine years old and posting for fun without any idea of what is printable. Models for education might or might not be accurate. So if you use one, be sure to review it and read the license that spells out how you are allowed to use it.

CREATIVE COMMONS LICENSES

3D-printing software and models are often released under a *creative commons license, which you might encounter* in the form of notations like "Released under a Creative Commons 4.0 International license, CC-BY-NC-SA," typically including a link to the relevant license text at www.creativecommons.org.

These licenses allow you to share your models or software freely while retaining some rights for yourself. The licenses are written in a somewhat modular fashion so you can add on restrictions to a basic license, shown by adding letter codes to the license name. A *CC-BY-NC-SA* license, for instance, allows anyone to do the following:

- Use your material (*CC*, creative commons)

- As long as they attribute it to you in a certain way (*BY*)

- And do not use it for commercial purposes (*NC*)

- And anyone who uses your materials must release their materials (including the part you contributed) under the same license (*SA*, for *share alike*)

Deciding how to release and use materials is complex, and you should consult a lawyer versed in software intellectual property if you are embarking on a major project, particularly if money and friendships are involved. The Creative Commons website is a good and lucid place to get some background first, though.

Many 3D printers have heritage to the RepRap project (www.reprap.org), which is an ongoing project to build an *open source* community of creative commons hardware and software. These printers are typically referred to as *open source printers.*

Tip   Chapter 5 includes a quick-start guide that talks you through how to create a small cube as a test. You can use that as a first test model and then move on to more complex things in Chapter 6. It may be tempting to download something from a repository and try that first, but if you have issues, you will not know if it is a printer problem or a model that has issues.

Scanning

Consumer-priced 3D scanners either require you to take multiple pictures from multiple angles or scan using a device that produces multiple laser beams or some other structured light pattern. Either way, you typically end up a lot of artifacts that have to be cleaned up manually in software, a process that can be tedious and time-consuming. Typically, people use a scan as a starting point for what they are doing or a dimensional reference and then draw over it in a CAD program to correct and clean up the scan. Software is the hard part of 3D scanning, and some professional scanners have software to automate some of this, but as of this writing these packages tend to cost many thousands of dollars. Figure 3-2 shows a 3D print of Rich, based on a scan made with a DIY scanner.

Tip   If you would like to build your own scanner, there are open source designs out there, like the Cyclop 3D scanner (an open hardware scanner for small objects built with 3D-printed parts that uses open source software) and Skanect (software that allows you to repurpose an Xbox Kinect for human-scale 3D scanning).

Figure 3-2. *Scanned and 3D printed sculpture*

Slicing Software: Filament Printers

3D printers cannot use a CAD output file (that is, an STL file) directly.
A piece of software known as a *slice engine* has to take the STL file and
figure out the commands that the 3D printer will execute a layer at a
time. Slice engines might be in freestanding programs, or combined with
other relevant software in the 3D-printing workflow. We call programs
containing one or more slice engines *slicing software*.

Tip   If you come into this from a machine-shop environment, slicing
software can also be thought of as computer-aided manufacturing
(CAM) software.

Slicing programs use different settings to allow for variations in the geometry of the printer, the type of filament you are using, and so on. Resin and other technologies are philosophically similar, but the differences are big enough that we talk about them in a different section of this chapter. In this section, we focus on filament printers.

There are many different slicing engines out there now. In most cases they are freestanding programs or code embedded in programs that are proprietary to a particular printer. Because getting all the settings right for a particular 3D printer can be fiddly, a lot of manufacturers modify one of these open source programs and create a proprietary program just for their machine. However, many printers can still use the basic open source program. We will describe several of those programs here, and go over some of the commonest 3D-printer settings and what they control.

Some of the more common, freely available programs are Slic3r, Cura, and MatterControl. Printers built around open source standards will often make a file of settings for one of these programs available, or create a custom program around one of these slicing engines.

Tip   Most slicing software allows you to simulate what the printer will do during your print with a graphic to step through the layers, and in some cases to simulate within a layer. Be sure to use this feature to walk through every print. It will save you a lot of grief and filament. We show some examples of this later in the chapter.

Slic3r

Slic3r (pronounced "slicer"—the 3 is silent) has been around for a long time and is maintained by an open source community led by Alessandro Ranellucci. Its slicing engine has been incorporated into other programs over time. Slic3r has a reputation for getting cutting-edge functionality first, which always has pluses and minuses. You can download it at www.slic3r.org.

MatterControl

MatterControl (www.mattercontrol.com) is a free program maintained by 3D printer retailer MatterHackers. As of this writing, it is in the process of a major upgrade to version 2.0. Version 1.x combined access to Slic3r, Cura, and its own slicing engine, MatterSlice. MatterControl 1.x is also a host program that allows users to send single commands to a printer, jog axes, and change extruder temperature. The update to 2.0 is planned to include a minimal CAD program as part of the front end, and a simplification to just its own slice engine.

Figure 3-3 is a screen shot of the current version (1.7). By the time you read this, it may be updated and generally available. Our book *3D Printing With Matter Control* (Apress, 2015) details the operation of version 1.x.

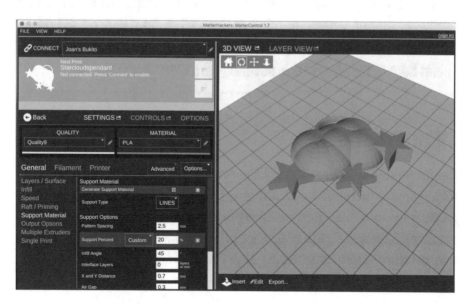

Figure 3-3. *Screen shot of MatterControl 1.7*

Ultimaker Cura 3

Utimaker Cura 3 is maintained as an open source program by 3D manufacturer Ultimaker, and can be downloaded from `https://ultimaker.com/en/products/ultimaker-cura-software`. In 2017 a major update to Cura 3.0 added many different control options to fine-tune prints. We will use Ultimaker Cura 3 for the rest of the screenshot examples in the "Using a Slicing Program" section of this chapter, with the kind permission of Ultimaker.

Note   In the past, Cura numbered its releases based on the year of release, ending in 2015 (Cura 15.x), and then changed numbering to Cura 2 and now Cura 3. Several 3D printer companies based their software on one version or other of Cura 15, so that version will be around for a while. Cura 15 is a lot simpler but very robust. The main point here is that Cura 15 is several years older than Cura 3.

Other Programs

The proliferation of 3D printers has been accompanied by a flurry of slicing programs. Some manufacturers (like Makerbot) have their own proprietary software. There are also printer-agnostic third-party programs out there, like Simplify3D, which is a powerful (but not free) program that also has some editing and mesh repair functions.

Using a Slicing Program

Slicing programs typically require that you give the program both some information about your 3D printer's geometry (the size of the print bed, whether it is heated or not, how tall a print can be, what size filament it uses, and so on). Often this is a file of some sort that your manufacturer will provide. If not, you will have to guesstimate as best you can. Failing that, you can always try the default settings in a slicer. Documentation on the download site for the slicing program you select should walk you through that. Once you have defined your printer, you will be facing the daunting list of settings to select.

Different programs may call similar settings by different names, and may change those names over time. We will not walk through step-by-step screen shots here, since by the time you read this they may well have changed. Instead, we will talk about the big groups of settings that you will need to think about, and what these settings do.

Example: Ultimaker Cura 3

We give a general introduction to slicer settings here using Ultimaker Cura 3. Like most slicing programs it requires you to input some information about your printer, then make some selections that are related to the material you are using, and then finally tweak some settings that might vary model to model.

Because there are dozens of settings (and because hovering over any setting in Custom mode gives you an explanation), we do not go through them exhaustively here. Rather, we suggest good ways to get started and then talk about exceptions and case studies in the later chapters of this book.

To get started, in the menus at the top of the opening screen, click Settings ➤ Printer ➤ Add Printer. Unless you have an Ultimaker, click Other to see if your make and model is listed. If not, click Custom. A first window labeled Printer will come up; input the dimensions (in millimeters) of your printer and whether or not it has a heated platform.

Then click the Extrude tab at the top of the window and input nozzle diameter and "compatible material diameter," which most other software would call "filament diameter." Start with either 2.85 for "3 millimeter" filament, or 1.75 for anything else. Save those settings, and then you will see a screen that looks something like Figure 3-4, but without a model displayed in the window.

To get started, drag an STL file into the window showing an empty platform. Figure 3-4 shows Recommended mode, which gives you a limited number of things to change. You can use the pulldown menu to select a material, and then select a layer height and whether or not to use support. Cura slices a file automatically each time you change something.

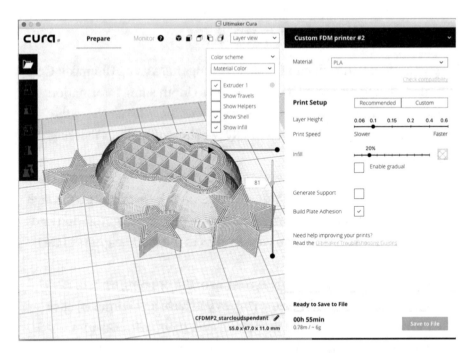

Figure 3-4. *Opening screen for Ultimaker Cura 3, basic setting*

Tip   We use the names of settings in Ultimaker Cura 3 in this discussion; if you use different software, the names might be a little different. Where similar settings have very different names in different common slicers, we will try to mention the other names you might want to look for. We have case studies scattered throughout the later chapters of this book. In this chapter we focus on the major slicer settings that you are likely to need to worry about often.

You may fairly rapidly decide you want to play with more of the settings. Select Custom to see more settings (Figure 3-5). If you know what a setting is called, you can search for it. Alternatively, you can click the gears next to each of the major categories to see more options; many settings are hidden by default, but clicking any gear lets you scroll around all settings. Hover your cursor over a setting to see what it does, and what else it affects. You can make a setting permanently visible by selecting what you want to have visible by default.

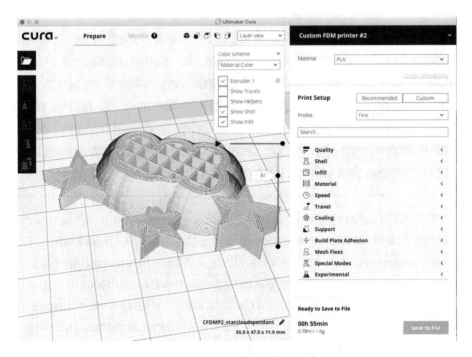

Figure 3-5. *Custom settings screen for Ultimaker Cura 3*

Simulating Your Print

You can see one of the most important tools in a slicer in Figures 3-4 and
3-5: the ability to simulate how your print will build up layer by layer. If you
select Layer View from the pulldown menu above your print, you will be
able to drag around sliders to move within a single layer, or from one layer
to the next. Even if you are an advanced 3D printer user, it is always a good
idea to walk quickly through a print to see if you forgot something, or if
something does not look remotely like you expected. In particular, look at
the very first layer of your object (the first layer beyond the raft, if you are
using a raft—see the discussion about rafts that follows) because if pieces
are missing, your print will likely fail.

Print Quality and Layer Height

3D printers print each layer in one plane parallel to the build platform and then step up and do the next layer. The extruder head moves upward, away from the platform, after completing each layer. The two axes in the plane of the platform are referred to as x and y, and the vertical axis is the z-axis, as we describe in Chapter 2. *Layer height* is defined as the thickness of the material in each step up of the z-axis. In Chapter 8 we discuss how to get as smooth a surface as possible.

Caution   Layer height has to be less than (not equal to!) the nozzle diameter. About 80% of the nozzle diameter is a good maximum value for layer height. Minimum layer height is not really dependent on the nozzle, and is determined by other factors. We talk more about layer height and surface smoothness in Chapter 8.

Shells

In an STL file, the surface is represented by a mesh of triangles. The slicer produces surfaces facing the sides with one or more perimeters around each layer, and surfaces facing up or down with solid layers (or solid areas of layers). The space inside this outer surface is then partially filled in to make the object stronger and to create a base for the next layer. The perimeters and solid areas are called the print's *shell*. The material that the slicing software will create for the interior support is called *infill*.

Your slicer will allow you to specify the thickness of the horizontal shell, either as a number of perimeters or in millimeters (which will be rounded to a multiple of your perimeter extrusion width). Two is typically a good number. The width (in the x-y plane) of this perimeter is the extrusion width, which must be no smaller than your nozzle diameter, and might be larger.

You can similarly set the thickness of the vertical shell, which your slicer might offer as a setting in millimeters or a number of top/bottom solid layers, or both. You will generally want at least three or four layers to avoid gaps. Setting the thickness in millimeters can be advantageous because it allows you to match your horizontal shell thickness when changing layer heights, and because very thin layers often have more trouble bridging over infill, so they may need the extra layers to smooth themselves out.

Platform Adhesion

One of the challenges with a 3D printer is getting the model to stick to the platform. Sometimes a model has a relatively small contact area with the platform, and when the extruder lays down the next layer it knocks the model loose. When that happens, the plastic that is intended to make up subsequent layers falls in random places as the structure gets knocked around. The resulting mess is typically called *printing hair* (in polite company, anyway). There are few worse feelings than smugly demonstrating a 3D printer to your friends and then noticing that your model is being merrily dragged around the platform, trailing strands of filament. Techniques to prevent such bad hair days follow.

Brims

A *brim* expands the first layer by creating additional perimeters to increase contact area with the platform, and is intended to be peeled away along the edge of the print's base. A brim usually is specified in terms of width away from the object. A few millimeters usually make a big difference. Figure 3-6 shows a brim stabilizing a print.

Note   Experts often make the first layer of a print a lot thicker than subsequent layers. A thick layer plus a brim can make it a lot more likely a print with a small contact area will survive to the end.

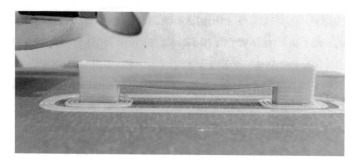

Figure 3-6. *A brim, skirt, and some bridging*

Skirts

A *skirt* is a few loops of filament laid down at the beginning of a print
that outline all the objects being printed at a given time and show the
maximum size of the first layer of the print. You can see one in Figure 3-6;
it is the double line that does not touch the print. A skirt can solve several
problems that might be encountered at the very start of a print.

It is possible to print more than one thing at a time on a 3D printer's
platform. The programs for arranging the objects for a print run show you
where the prints will be positioned relative to each other. However, it is
always possible to create something that would wind up too big to print,
since the (virtual) version can be hanging off the platform. When the skirt
is drawn around all the objects that you are planning on printing, it allows
you to quickly see whether there are any problems so you can stop the
print right away.

Also, if you have just switched filaments from one color to another, it
is good to print something away from your object first so that any material
of a different color that is still in the nozzle is melted out before starting to
print the main object. Plastic may also ooze out of the nozzle after a print,
or while heating up for the next one, which can leave a void that causes
a delay before plastic starts coming out again. Generally, a skirt allows
the printer to finish filling the extruder with filament (known as *priming*)
before the main object starts printing.

The skirt is usually a few millimeters away from the location on the platform where the first layer of the main object being printed will reside. By the time a few loops are done, any previous filament should also be flushed out of the nozzle. Most programs allow the user to specify both the distance that the skirt is from the main model and the number of loops constituting the skirt.

Tip   Add a few loops to the skirt when you change to a light-colored filament after printing a previous print with a dark filament. Doing so clears out the nozzle so there will not be any mixing of colors and resulting staining of your print.

Rafts

When you look at the lists of settings in a slicing program you may see options for a raft. A *raft* is a few layers of support material underneath a print. In the early days of 3D printing, when beds were often uneven and there were no heated platforms, rafts could help prints stick better. This practice has largely gone out of favor since a good first layer and perhaps a brim are a better combination on a modern printer.

A raft is a good solution if a print does not have many contact points with the bed and you want to be sure it will not fall off—for example, a large object that you do not want to fail midway through a 12-hour print. Rafts are also useful if you need the bottom surface to be dimensionally accurate, since direct contact with an uneven platform can leave it slightly skewed or not entirely flat.

The bottom layer of a raft is printed with extrusion lines that are not only taller than a normal layer, but wider so that they have more contact area with the platform. The larger volume of plastic being pushed out of the nozzle also makes the print less sensitive to being a little too far from the platform surface in some areas, whereas having the nozzle further from the surface reduces the risk of jamming the extruder or even damaging the nozzle or the platform by getting too close in others.

Modern slicers give you the ability to do this without a raft by using a setting called "initial layer line width" or "first layer extrusion width." In conjunction with the initial layer height setting, this allows you to configure the first layer of your print to stick like a raft's base layer, without the added time or wasted plastic. Because you will be putting out a lot more plastic at once, it a good idea to slow this layer down significantly if you are going to use these features, to prevent jams, and slower printing is good for first layer adhesion anyway. If you are using these features and decide that a print needs a raft, be sure to set them closer to your normal printing settings—otherwise you will be increasing adhesion to the raft, and you may not be able to get it off!

Supporting and Orienting a Model

Consumer 3D printers build up their models from a platform, whether the extruder is fixed and the platform drops away or the extruder head moves up and away from a platform. This means that in some cases, a print head would be laying down material in air. For example, imagine a statue with an outstretched arm. Assuming that the statue is being printed up from its base, the initial bottom layers of the arm would print into the air and fall down unless something was printed into the open space all the way up from the platform. Material printed like this is called *support*. Sometimes this problem can be minimized or eliminated altogether by printing the model in a different orientation. This section talks about these interacting considerations.

Support

In a 3D print, the first layer sticks to the platform. Then the second layer is added above that, and so on, like a brick wall. The printer depends on having something below the nozzle to compress the extrusion against, much like the mortar between bricks. In the case of the wall, if there are no bricks under the second layer (or at least some bricks partially lapped under it), the second layer of brick will fall to the ground. If you want to lay bricks across the top of an opening in the wall, like a window or doorway, you need a scaffolding to support them as you are building. (For exceptions to this, see the section on bridging later in this chapter.)

In 3D printing, the structures that prevent the equivalent problem are called *support* (Figure 3-7). The slicing process generates support automatically in some programs, and with some user control in others. In general, it is best to avoid support if possible because removing it is time-consuming and the process of pulling it off can damage the model. Unless you are using a second soluble print material as support, you will then need to remove the support mechanically. You may need needle-nosed pliers, a screwdriver, and ultimately tweezers or other small tool to take off the last bits, as discussed in Chapter 5 (plus some eye protection—those bits can be sharp).

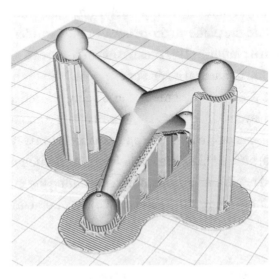

Figure 3-7. *A model with support*

Orientation

A particular model may seem to have a side that is "supposed" to be the bottom of the model. Sometimes, though, turning a model so that it lies on its side or even upside-down can increase the first-layer contact with the platform and decrease the amount of support. Particularly if you are going to be printing the object more than once, spending some time playing with the orientation of a complex model is worthwhile.

A bit of thought can sometimes also eliminate support that the slicing software would automatically create in hard-to-get-at places, like internal narrow spaces. Sometimes turning a complicated object through some arbitrary rotation—for example, 10 degrees about the x-axis, and 15 degrees about the y-axis —will result in the best situation with the least support needed.

Printers that can only use one filament at a time print support in the same material as the rest of the model. Printers that have multiple extruders can lay a dissolvable filament, though this process is often more costly, time-consuming, and error-prone than using your print material.

In addition to not needing supports, surfaces that are close to vertical will have less obvious layer lines than ones that are close to horizontal, because the distance along the surface from one layer line to the next is shorter. This makes the surface appear smoother and allows fine details in the design to show (some of which the slicer might otherwise have to omit because they are less than two extrusions wide), so you should consider this as well when reorienting a model. Figure 3-8 shows a print that was created vertically (gravitational waves, from our 2017 Apress book, *3D Printed Science Projects, Volume 2*).

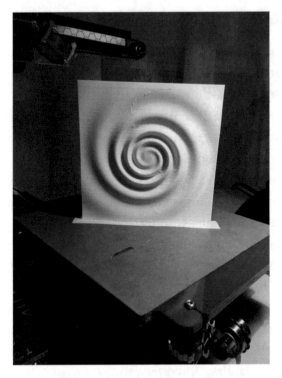

Figure 3-8. *Gravitational wave model, printed vertically*

Avoiding Support by Cutting a Model into Pieces

For an object with a complex surface that requires support, sometimes you can cut the object into two or more pieces, print the pieces cut-side-down, and then glue the parts together later. Some CAD programs have tools to make this sort of cut. If the program you are using does not, there are a few free or open source programs that allow the user to rotate an object around all three axes and then make a cut along a resulting convenient axis. Because this is a rapidly evolving area, search online for "cutting STL files free software." Often printed support can be avoided entirely with one judicious cut. After printing, the halves will have to be glued together. Chapter 8 discusses paint, glue, and finishing.

Managing Internal Open Space

Just as there is open space around the outside of a model (like the statue's outstretched arm mentioned earlier) similar problems arise inside a model or in space enclosed by a model. Imagine a closed box: it would need some sort of support to run between the top and bottom. This support is called *infill*. Sometimes it is not necessary to have infill everywhere, and you can get away with just stringing filament across (usually) small gaps, a process called *bridging*. This section gives you some ideas about the design issues that arise with internal support.

Bridging

It is possible to bridge across open areas in a model without support if the open area is not too wide (say, less than 20–30 mm, depending on your printer's cooling fans and other factors). There are several schools of thought about the best settings to use when bridging across a gap. On the one hand, having the printer move more slowly than usual while trying to increase filament flow rate slightly may result in the bridge sagging a little. Conversely, having the printer move faster and push out less may mean the filament will not stretch enough to cross the open area and will break. Finding an optimum between the two requires some experimentation with your printer.

Some slicing programs have settings for adjusting speed and flow of plastic specifically for bridging. Defaulting these settings to the rate the slicing program creates is a good place to start.

Another way to get around bridging is to terrace or arc under the bridged area so that the printer is in fact just climbing a 45-degree (or shallower) slope underneath. An overhang climbing at about a 45-degree angle is about the limit that can be consistently printed without support. However, sometimes a steeper slope will work with some combinations of settings; a bit of experimentation is often worthwhile to avoid needing to use support, particularly in a complex structure. If bridges are too long, though, as with the print in Figure 3-6, the bridge may sag a bit or have drooled bits of filament on it.

Infill

Users of 3D printers do not usually want to create solid objects, because that uses a lot of filament. However, typically objects cannot be hollow, either, because upper layers would be printed in air. (Exceptions to this are discussed in Chapter 8.) As a result, most slicing software creates internal support called *infill* inside the solid surfaces of an object to minimize filament use (as well as to make the print faster). Figure 3-9 shows typical infill patterns.

Another purpose of using infill patterns (as opposed to printing solid plastic), and possibly the most important one for some materials, is to control shrinkage. Infill patterns are sparse enough to stretch axially as they shrink radially so that they do not pull the perimeters inward as they cool and shrink. This can make 3D-printed parts maintain dimensional accuracy much better than injection-molded parts, which have to be designed with a significantly different size and shape from the final part in order to turn out the way the designer intends after shrinkage.

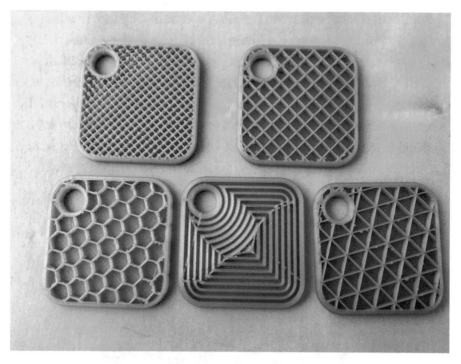

Figure 3-9. *Typical infill patterns*

Print infill is usually specified in terms of percentage fill. So, 12% infill means that 12% of the interior volume of the object will be occupied by material and 88% will be open. (This percentage does not include the outer perimeter of the print.)

Although infill adds some strength by bracing the interior of the object against collapsing, most of the print's strength comes from the solid surfaces, and if you want to make a print stronger, it is usually better to increase the thickness of the skin rather than increasing infill. Compared to printing completely hollow, infill is more important for its ability to act as a support structure for a model's internal overhangs, to prevent sagging or gaps in the top surface of a print. Most slicers have some more exotic options for infill patterns, but unless you are printing with a highly transparent filament, these patterns are unlikely to be visible once the print has finished.

For the best results with top surfaces, you want a pattern that is very regular and not too sparse where it meets that surface, since overly large gaps often result either in sagging or *pillowing* between infill lines (Figure 3-10). *Pillowing* occurs when instead of drooping downward where it is unsupported by infill, the plastic curls upward, and it is an especially common failure mode when printing thinner layers. Adding more solid top layers helps to even these surfaces out, but for very small prints, you may find that this uses more plastic than just using a higher infill density.

Figure 3-10. *Pillowing on a 20 mm cube*

Although there are now some infill patterns that are designed to create 3D structures within a model, most are the same every layer or print in different directions on alternating layers. This means that the shape and size of the gaps between lines will be consistent when they intersect with the top and bottom surfaces. But why do those surfaces need to be solid? If you think of a square filled with a grid of squares, it would be fairly easy to crush that shape by applying force to opposite corners. You can brace it with a triangular grid instead, but filling the front and back faces is even more effective, so strength is rarely a big factor in the choice of infill patterns.

There is such a thing as a print created without top and bottom solid layers. Vase mode prints (Chapter 8) omit the infill and top layers to turn a solid model into a vessel that is open on top.

Note   Printing solid (100% infill) is a special case, and we discuss the issues and printer settings relevant to that in Chapter 8.

Retraction and Stringing

One of the big advantages of 3D printing is that complex shapes that might be impossible to create via traditional machining can often be made very easily on a 3D printer. But there are some features that are challenging to 3D print—with a consumer printer, anyway. For example, one thing that can be difficult to print is an object with two skinny towers. To "leave out" the space between the towers, the extruder needs to pump out material to make one tower, stop extruding, and start up again on the other tower. This is referred to as *retraction*. When retraction is not adequate, the print may have fine hairs of filament scattered across the spaces that were supposed to be open; this is referred to as *stringing (Figure 3-11)*.

Figure 3-11. Stringing

Retraction is typically handled as an automatic feature in slicing software with some limited user control. In Cura, there are many settings to fine-tune retraction under the Material heading. Also, in the Travel section, you can tick a box to allow *combing*. This is a way to avoid retracting if printing sparse or complex infill might otherwise require it. It does not matter if infill strings a bit, because it will only be visible inside the model when the model is complete. Doing a lot of retraction can wear on the filament in some printer configurations and slows down the printing process, so avoiding it where possible is a big plus.

Temperatures

You may find that you need to tweak settings as you print in different materials. The temperature of your extruder (and your heated build platform, if yours has a heater) will vary with the materials. In Chapter 2 we talked about the requirements for several common materials. The reality is that every time you use a new brand (or even color) of filament, you may need to experiment a bit.

In Cura 3, temperatures are under the Materials section. There are a bunch of temperatures you can change, but to start just make them all the same as each other. Filament spools usually suggest a temperature range. In the absence of other information from your experience or manufacturer, just start in the middle of the range. Too hot can result in stringing or blobby prints; too cool can result in poor adhesion between layers and the platform or between two layers.

Be sure that your nozzle and platform can handle the temperature you are asking them to reach. Printers have very limited error checking, and it is possible to damage your printer by telling components to get hotter than they are rated for.

Speeds, Cooling, Extrusion Multipliers

Your slicer will include several settings for speeds of a print. Unless the slicer specifies otherwise, all of its speeds are speeds of linear motion. This is the maximum speed that the printer will move for this portion of the print, but acceleration my not allow it to reach that speed, and cooling settings may also limit it.

Travel speeds control how fast the printer moves when it is moving between parts without extruding. This should generally be set as fast as the machine can handle, since going slower will not only increase print time, it will allow more time for plastic to ooze out of the nozzle in areas where you do not want it.

Most slicers also include several different printing speeds. Perimeters, infill, and solid surfaces all generally have their own printing speeds. You may be tempted to speed up your print by printing the infill quickly and slowing down the outer perimeters to get smoother motion—be careful, because residual pressure in the nozzle might cause a blob where the perimeter starts. The one place it is always good to set a slower speed is for the first layer, because slowing it down helps with platform adhesion and reduces the chances of something bad happening if the platform is not aligned perfectly.

In Cura 3, the Minimum Layer Time setting tells the slicer to reduce speeds if a layer will take less than the specified time to complete. This is done to allow time for the plastic to cool before printing another layer on top of it. If the plastic does not cool sufficiently, you can get a misshapen blob of plastic instead of the fine features of your model. There are also settings to control the speed of fans pointed down at your print. Depending on the strength of your fans, you may be able to cool the plastic faster, allowing lower values for minimum layer time to be used.

If your print has a single narrow feature at the top, minimum layer time might not be able to do its job because the plastic stays in contact with the hot nozzle and does not have a chance to cool. In this case, printing two of your object at once or adding a cylinder the same height as your print (known as a *cooling tower*) will give the printer something else to do so that it moves away from that feature and allows it to cool properly.

The speed at which plastic is pushed out is controlled by the combination of this speed and the specified layer height and extrusion width according to a calculation of volume. The slicer needs to know the diameter of the filament so it knows how much volume of plastic is in one millimeter of it. If this calculation results in the wrong volume of plastic, usually because the extruder is not properly calibrated, the Flow setting, otherwise known as an Extrusion Multiplier, gives you a fudge factor to tweak this calculation.

More Exotic Settings

Settings often interact with each other, and the details of a particular case matter. We have relegated talking about some of the more exotic options—like printing vases or printing solid, transparent objects—to the case studies in Chapter 8, where we discuss arts applications.

Troubleshooting

Troubleshooting a print that does not look right is a complex subject. In this chapter we are summarizing some of the big categories of slicer settings. In later chapters we will go over some case studies and go into more depth for particular types of prints there. Table 3-1 shows a quick guide to where to find solutions to different types of issues.

Tip   Joan and Rich have courses on Lynda.com/LinkedIn Learning that go into greater detail on these topics. You can find them by going to Lynda.com and searching on our names.

Table 3-1. *Quick Guide to Slicer Settings*

Problem	Likely Group of Settings that Will Fix It	Chapter Where Discussed
Print does not stick to bed	Temperature	3
	Bed surface/raft, brim	2 and 3
	Support	3
Gaps in print	Extrusion settings	3
Surface quality	Layer height, speeds, cooling	3 and 8
Blobby prints	Cooling, or print too tall and thin	3 and 8
Stringing	Retraction	3

Printing More Than One Object at a Time

Most slicers will allow you to put multiple objects from different STLs on the platform and print them all at once. Typically, this works by printing all of them in parallel. The first layers of all parts are printed before the second layer of any part starts.

Some slicers offer a sequential printing option as well, which allows you to print one object and then print another on an unused part of the print bed. This requires careful arrangement, though, to ensure that no other part of the printer will collide with the parts that have already been completed. This prevents you from using as much of the space as you can when printing all at once.

Multiple Extruders

A printer with more than one extruder allows you to print in multiple colors or materials. Exactly how this works depends a lot on the multiple-extruder machine in question, but this general guide will give you some ideas on how to get started with your machine. This usually does not mean you can print faster, since only one extruder can be active at once (though as of this writing, there are experimental machines that are designed to work this way, based on Autodesk's Project Escher). Rather, a printer with multiple extruders usually cannot move them entirely independently, so only one can be used at a time.

Some machines have multiple nozzles mounted to a single toolhead so that they move together, and simply offset the toolhead's position when they are using one nozzle or the other. Others use various types of splitter mechanisms to run filament from several different extruder mechanisms through a common nozzle. Still others have somewhat independent motion that allows one extruder to be parked to one side of the machine while the other is working. One company, Mosaic Manufacturing, even sells an add-on device that cuts and splices filament before feeding it to the printer.

Printers that use a single nozzle are generally only useful for printing multiple colors, since materials with different properties usually need different printing temperatures, and may not play well with the switching mechanisms. Though some attempts have been made at color mixing, most of these are only able to switch filaments automatically, so creating a gradient of color usually is not possible. Single-nozzle solutions usually result in a lighter toolhead that can handle high acceleration better than multi-nozzle ones, and have the advantage of avoiding ooze from the inactive nozzle and various alignment issues.

Those with multiple extruders, each with their own nozzle, can use the second one to print a soluble support material, or a flexible material to have a mixture of print properties. Some of these also have software that allows them to be used in duplication mode, where two identical objects (which must be smaller than the distance between the nozzles) are printed simultaneously.

If the machine is able to move the two extruders independently in one axis (known as independent dual extruder, or IDEX, machines), their duplication mode can usually use half of the platform for each copy. However, multiple nozzles on a single carriage are usually situated as close as possible to one another, leading to much stricter limits on these modes. Some IDEX printers even have a mirror duplication mode, in which the motion of the independent axis is reversed to create copies that are mirror images of one another (like a pair of shoes).

One common use of dual-extruder machines is to use one of the extruders to print support material that can be dissolved away later. To use one of these systems for dissolvable support, you need to configure the slicer to print its support with a different extruder, and make sure that extruder has appropriate settings for your support material.

When you are printing models in two colors (or two materials), you need to follow a somewhat different process than printing dissolvable support, or printing in one material. To do this, you need to create two STL files that represent the areas of the print that are to be printed with each color.

You also have to split your model into two STL files so that there are no places with structure created with both colors trying to occupy the space. If something penetrates something else, there must be a hole in the one object to accommodate the second, just as in physical space. These files then need to be interleaved into an .AMF file. Note that any rotation needed when arranging the files for printing has to be done in the STL file generation. We walk through an example in detail in Chapter 6.

Tip   If you are using a dual-extruder 3D printer to print two colors and, on top of that, support is needed, you will need to pick one of the extruders to do the support for both materials.

Mesh Repair Programs

Sometimes a mesh (the type of data found in an STL file) comes into the slicing program with issues, and the sliced file does not look like you would expect. Some CAD programs create models that are not watertight (the boundary of the shape would not hold water because it has holes in it). Some models are not *manifold*, which means that two parts of the model in the computer are trying to occupy the same physical space. This is not a problem in a computer model, but can have unexpected results when the slicer program tries to reconcile conflicts into something that will work physically. If your model does weird things when you slice it, you might need to repair the mesh.

There are several programs that work well to repair meshes, or to reduce the number of triangles that make up the mesh surface. Sometimes a model can be computationally so big that it can overwhelm the program, and you need to cut down (*decimate*, in the lingo) on the number of triangles. Sometimes, too, you want to cut a model in half to make it easier to print, and then glue it together. Some mesh repair programs let you do that, too.

The venerable Meshlab (www.meshlab.net) is an open source, very powerful program. But it is not particularly intuitive, although its 2016 update has a good web page with some instructions. To clean up a mesh, open the program and click File ➤ Import Mesh to bring in your STL file. Then just agree to its cleanup suggestions and use File ➤ Export as to send it back out it again (be sure to select STL, which is not the default).

To use it to decimate a mesh, click Filters ➤ Remeshing, Simplification and Reconstruction ➤ Simplification: Quadric Edge Collapse Decimation, which we are sure you would have guessed on your own. Then you can see how many vertices all the triangles add up to and suggest a smaller number. Or in the box Percentage reduction type a number between 0 and 1 to reduce it—typing 0.5 drops the number of vertices by 50%. Click the Apply button to have your changes take effect. The program will display what it did. If you like it, you can use File ➤ Export As to save your changes. If not, just abandon the effort and start over.

If the free software is not enough for you, you can look into Simplify3D (described earlier in this chapter) or Netfabb (`www.autodesk.com/products/netfabb/overview`). Chapter 6 also discusses how to create good meshes in the first place.

G-code

Most open source, filament-using 3D printers are controlled with a series of commands, called *G-code*. G-code loads onto the printer from a host computer via USB port, wifi, or other network connection, or is read from an SD card or USB drive, depending on which options a particular machine has. The *firmware* (software running on the printer itself) then interprets the G-code one command at a time and controls the hardware functions needed to execute it. Status information (temperatures and the like) returns to the user's computer through the USB. In some other cases, a G-code interpreter runs on a host computer, and control signals are sent to the printer.

Many open source printers use Marlin firmware, which runs on Arduino-compatible microcontrollers. There is no operating system running on a microcontroller in system architectures like the Arduino.

The processing hardware performs minimal command retrieval buffering and interpretation functions, and returns requested signals to the user. There are variations on this theme: for example, some printers can read from an SD card rather than needing to use a USB port.

G-code is a very old programming language originally designed to control machine tools with a computer. Its origins are in the 1950s and 1960s and it has survived this long because of its flexibility and ability to run with minimal computing power. G-code is very low-level and is typically written such that all the commands are interpreted one at a time sequentially. Typical G-code functions include commanding an extruder to heat up to a particular temperature, instructing the printer to pause until an extruder reaches a certain temperature, moving the extruder to some (x, y, z) position, and conducting similar activities.

G-code for machine tools evolved gradually, with different dialects for each tool manufacturer. A standard of sorts called RS274D stabilized in the mid-1980s. Because the computer numerical control (CNC) market was pretty stable when the first low-cost 3D printers came along, a lot of the early users borrowed firmware and concepts to program those machines, and so a G-code dialect for 3D printers developed.

Each line of G-code commands the printer to do some small task or to set some parameter to a value that will be used for a task later on. For example, the snippet of code in the example that follows first sets the units that the firmware will use for calculation to millimeters (G21). It then tells the firmware to use absolute, not relative, coordinates (G90). The G1(...) command advances the extruder to position (3.000, 8.111, 4.444). During that move, 0.1234 mm of filament will have extruded, relative to the last time the zero point was reset; resets occur periodically during a print. (Retractions are negative E values.)

```
G21
G90
G1 X3.000 Y8.111 Z4.444 E0.1234
```

The firmware interpolates the movements required to get from one absolute position to the next and similarly determines how to feed the filament to extrude the requested amount before the next step. Millimeters of filament moved is currently the most common unit for the E values, but some machines have begun the switch to units of volume instead.

Not all G-codes begin with G. For example, codes beginning with M are used (with some variation among manufacturers) for most functions that are not directly related to movement of the axes. M104 is commonly used in open source printers to set the extruder temperature to a particular value. M140 sets the temperature of heated build platforms—in the example following this paragraph, to 115 degrees C. M109 waits for the temperature of the extruder to reach the specified level, and M190 waits for the temperature of the heated platform to reach the specified temperature. (Note that though the code is usually written as shown in the example, M109 and M190 do not need to have a temperature specified. If none is given, then the temperature that was set with M140 and M104 commands will be used.)

Tip   Each line of G-code needs to be on one line (no newlines). A semicolon on the line makes the rest of the line a comment (see the example that follows).

```
M104 S210 ;comments here
M140 S115
M109 S210
M190 S115
```

Printers with multiple extruders need to address lines of G-code to the correct extruder. This is done with a *tool change* command, T. For example, in the case of most open source dual-extruder printers, T0 will select the first extruder, and T1 will select the second extruder (following the common computing convention of beginning to count at zero). A T0 code will cause everything that follows to be executed on extruder 1. Some G-codes allow a Tx to be appended on the same line to show that just that command is for extruder x.

Tip   A list of 3D-printer G-codes and a detailed discussion of their functions is available at `http://reprap.org/wiki/G-code`.

In Chapter 5, we discuss how it is sometimes useful to be able to type in these low-level codes to debug possible hardware failures (such as blocked extruders or lack of connection to the printer) or to change the G-code built by your slicing program. Sometimes it is convenient to test that the printer is working correctly with a few simple commands rather than a complex G-code file.

Host Programs

Programs that give you an interactive interface to control your 3D printer are called *host programs*. They allow you to upload a whole file of G-code commands to create a print, or to send single commands when that is needed. Most 3D printers have a USB port that allows you to connect them to software running on a computer to stream instructions in real time. This is useful for manual control (used for maintenance operations, for instance), but it is not the best way to run a long-running print. If the computer goes to sleep, or you move your laptop and the cable comes out, hours of printing can be wasted.

Today, most printers have an option to store G-code (or whatever format the printer uses for its instructions) on the printer so that it can run untethered. Most often, this is done with an SD card (or microSD), though there are now some printers that use a USB stick or have onboard storage that you can upload to via a wifi connection. It is possible to upload to an SD card over USB, but for complex prints, that can take several hours because the protocols that 8-bit microcontrollers use for USB and SD card access are much slower than the ones your computer uses to communicate with the SD card directly. If your printer uses an SD card, you will want to take the card out and transfer files to it directly from your computer. Those that have wifi usually have faster protocols, but it may still be faster to move the SD card.

Many slicing programs have a limited host functionality to allow you to either save a G-code file to an SD card or upload it to a printer. Some allow you to send single-command controls to move an axis and so on, and others are limited to just uploading. MatterControl and Ultimaker Cura (discussed earlier) allow both.

Octoprint

If your printer only has USB, or if you really want wifi control but your printer did not come with it, there is an option. Octoprint (`www.octoprint.org`) is a printer host program that is accessed through a web interface, and it also has an API that many desktop host programs now support. It is designed to run on a computer without a keyboard or monitor that is permanently connected to the printer's USB. Although it is possible to run the Octoprint server on a Mac or Windows PC, it is designed to run on inexpensive single-board computers like the Raspberry Pi.

Resin Printers

There is surprisingly little commonality between printing with filament and with plastic. Within resin printers, too, there are some big differences between the two major technologies: SLA cures the resin one small spot at a time. DLP cures an entire layer at a time. Typically, the laser for either one shines in through an optical window at the bottom of a tray of resin, and a layer forms on the window. The window is then mechanically separated from the print by moving the print, the tray, or some combination to separate them.

Support is still necessary with a resin print. However, most print upside-down, so support is needed both to keep the print adhering correctly to the platform, and to resist the forces encountered when the print is peeled off the window. One might think that a print should just be printed upside-down from the way you would print it with filament, but it is more complex than that.

The first layer is tricky, because there is very little room between the platform and the optical window. Often people orient their resin prints to rest (upside-down) on top of a bed of thin support with a sacrificial solid layer on the build platform.

Another issue that makes slicing resin prints tricky is that exposure time and other parameters can depend critically on the characteristics of the resin. This and the fact that creating support is more challenging to think about have resulted in many resin printers having proprietary interfaces. Formlabs has a software package called PreForm, for instance. A screenshot of a print with typical support is shown in Figure 3-12. PreForm allows you to create custom supports too if the defaults are not exactly what you wanted. Note that this is the same model shown (with filament-printer supports) in Figure 3-7, so you can do some comparisons.

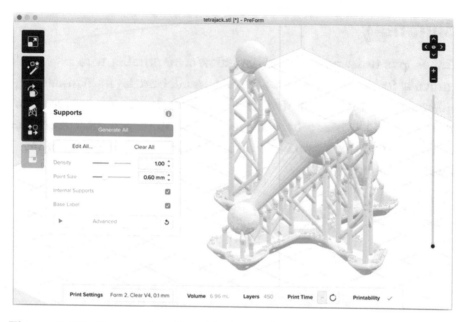

Figure 3-12. *Screen shot from PreForm (courtesy of Formlabs)*

When printing in a liquid, you also have to worry about bubbles forming. If any air gets trapped in the print as it forms, that can result in *voids* in the print since nothing will harden there. Prints have to be designed and oriented carefully to allow a way for air to escape.

For DLP printers that do not have proprietary software, there are a few options, notably Datatree3D's Creation Workshop (needs a paid license fee, `https://datatree3d.com/software/`). Alternatively, NanoDLP (`www.nanodlp.com/download/`) runs on a Raspberry Pi and is free to users.

Summary

This chapter reviewed the overall workflow of 3D printing, with a particular focus on the process of slicing a model into layers. It discussed different software packages that are available for the process, and some of the many settings that are available to tweak for the best print. The chapter focused primarily on filament-based 3D printers, with a summary of key difference for resin printers.

PART II

Living with Your 3D Printer

Part II (Chapters 4–6) review how to decide what kind of printer you need to buy, based on what you want to build with it and what materials you think you will want to be able to use. This part also reviews what kinds of facilities different 3D printers require and offers hands-on details of dealing with issues that might arise during a print. Finally, this part reviews options that you can use to create 3D-printable model files.

CHAPTER 4

Selecting a Printer: Comparing Technologies

There are now hundreds of different models of 3D printer on the market. But how do you even start to think about which one to buy? In this chapter, we will look at what 3D printer features are likely to be important for your intended uses, and also discuss how to estimate the long-term cost of ownership.

Because 3D printer models (and even manufacturers) come and go on a pretty regular basis, we will avoid suggesting particular models. Once you know what you are looking for, you can be a more skeptical reader of advertisements. You can also be more confident that you will purchase what you will need.

In Chapter 2 we review different types of 3D printer hardware, and in Chapter 3, of software. Refer back to those chapters if you are not sure about terminology. We cover selected hardware decisions here in the context of deciding what to purchase, but you should read the prior two chapters first for the full details of what part of the printer does what.

In Chapter 5, we talk about what happens when you bring the printer into its new home. That should drive your buying decisions, too. The space your printer will live in, who will maintain it, and how often you intend to move it are things you should think about before settling on a model.

© Joan Horvath, Rich Cameron 2018
J. Horvath and R. Cameron, *Mastering 3D Printing in the Classroom, Library, and Lab*,
https://doi.org/10.1007/978-1-4842-3501-0_4

Who Is Your User?

The first thing to consider with a printer purchase is how it will be used.
If it is going to be in a home office and used occasionally by one adult,
obviously it will not need to be as robust as if it is going to be in a room full
of kids.

Most 3D printers are labeled for ages 13 and up, and on average that is
probably about when it makes sense to let kids run them. There are a few
that are marketed specifically for kids to use directly, but those machines
needed to make tradeoffs to be able to do that (limiting functionality) that
might or might not make sense. Typically, an adult will manage the printer
hardware for the younger set because there are hot moving parts involved.

Before your purchase, imagine a day in the life of the printer and
have that scenario in mind as you read through this chapter and Chapter 5.
Many academic labs have huge pulses in use around deadlines, so
consider both your routine periods and your peak weeks.

3D Printer Resolution

When you buy a conventional printer to print on paper, you can note a few
familiar metrics about how good the image quality will be, often stated
in dots per inch (dpi). However, in the case of a 3D printer, it is a little
more complicated. You are dealing with somewhat different processes
in the cross-layer direction (usually vertically, the z-axis) versus the two
dimensions in the plane of the build platform (x- and y-axes).

3D printers often quote their resolution in the z-axis (the vertical one)
as a number in millimeters (or microns—one millimeter is 1,000 microns);
this is equivalent to the thinnest layer the printer can produce. Typically,
this number is better (smaller) than the feature size in the x-y plane. It also
is a good proxy for how smooth the surface will be. For most filament-based
3D-printing technologies, resolution is typically on the order of 0.1 mm,

or 100 microns. For practical reasons, such as the fact that smaller layers require a longer print time, going that low can be challenging. Beyond about 0.1 mm, the print time increase is usually much more noticeable than the difference in quality, so even if your printer claims 0.05 mm resolution or better, for practical reasons, you will usually end up using 0.1 mm or larger layers.

For 3D printers that use plastic filament, that plastic is being heated and squeezed out of a nozzle that is typically about half a millimeter in diameter. This string of plastic can be compressed between the nozzle and the previous layer down to that 0.1 mm thickness (or even smaller) in the z direction, but in the x-y plane it cannot be thinner than the diameter of the nozzle. The printer's control over the *placement* of these lines is much finer though—usually significantly better than 0.1 mm.

Comparisons of claims about resolution in the x-y plane for these machines are mostly meaningless because of the way the motors are controlled and how that interacts with extrusion on small scales.

Furthermore, the shape of each layer must be enclosed by a perimeter that is a closed loop, so features need to be at least two extrusion widths thick in that plane, or about 1 mm across. (There are exceptions to this through software that allows you to create single-width sections, but as a practical matter you may not want to.) So, you may find that your "50 micron" printer really is limited to features about 20 times that big, just because that resolution does not really apply in all three dimensions!

Figure 4-1 shows how thick layers (in the foreground) might not be able to fill a curved surface completely compared to thinner ones. The real benefit of higher resolution (of thinner layers) is that the deviations from a smooth surface where one layer transitions to the next are smaller. All other things being equal, this means that a higher resolution print has smoother surfaces with sharper edges. Corners in the x-y plane still will not have a radius smaller than half the nozzle diameter, though. Thus, whether a finer resolution actually makes smaller features visible depends on the print's orientation with respect to the x-y plane, as you can see in Figure 4-1.

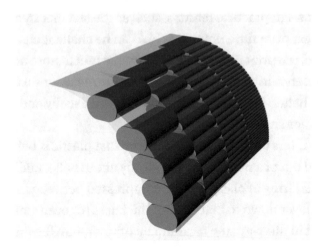

Figure 4-1. *Resolution showing effects of layer thickness*

Selecting a Printer

Two of the most critical questions when you are thinking about buying a 3D printer are who is going to use it, and what they are going to use it for. Art projects and robotics teams have different materials needs, for example. In later chapters, we go into this in some depth for different types of users, but here we will summarize the aspects that affect a purchasing decision. We have organized this section around the choices of features that you need to make when buying a 3D printer.

Filament vs. Resin

The main choice facing most educational and scientific users is whether to buy a 3D printer that uses spools of plastic as a raw material, or one that uses liquid resin. Filament printers are still far more prevalent and diverse, so we focus on them more here. A filament printer will be more practical for most users because the raw material is relatively easy to store and transport, and there is very little waste. The main drawback with a filament printer is that, as noted in the discussion of resolution, the smallest feature you can print is about twice your nozzle diameter—about a millimeter for typical 0.35 to 0.5 mm nozzles. That is plenty fine enough resolution for many things, but it is usually a little too coarse for jewelry or other delicate structures.

Resin printers (which come in several types, as discussed in Chapter 2) can create prints with smaller feature sizes since they are only really limited by the spot size of a laser or the pixel size of a projector. Print volume, though, also tends to be correspondingly small, and except for exotic, very expensive technologies, resin printing is significantly slower than filament printing (individual layers might be faster, but those layers are usually thinner, requiring more of them to print a given part).

The resin and the cleanup chemicals are messy and will have to be managed and disposed of. If you can handle that and you are looking at doing sophisticated projects that require fine detail, you may want to explore resin printers. If in doubt, buy a low-cost filament printer and get some experience there first.

We are going to assume in this chapter that if you want to go to the more sophisticated technologies described in Chapter 2, you will have good reasons and a specialized problem to solve. We will not explore powder-based, composite, and the more expensive and exotic technologies in the purchase tradeoffs in this chapter.

Time to Print

3D printers build up objects one layer at time. Typically, this layer is about as thick as one or two sheets of paper. This means that 3D prints take a long time. Often 3D printers are purchased by people with little or no exposure to traditional manufacturing, and the expectation is that the print will pop off the platform in the time it takes to print a page with ink. Making anything with a subtractive tool takes surprisingly long, too; precise manufacture of physical things is just inherently slow. Think how long it takes to build a brick wall, or for that matter, to paint a mural on one.

Tip   Print times will drive a lot of your workflow and probably narrow the types of projects that will be feasible in a school or library environment. A fist-sized print may take from several hours to a day to print, depending on a lot of things. As we note later in this section, smaller printers are often faster, if the thing you want to make will fit in the smaller build volume.

Selecting a Filament-Based 3D Printer

For most educational users, the basic decision will be which filament-based 3D printer to purchase, so we will focus most of our analysis on that topic in the following sections. For a discussion of the different types of resin printers on the market as of this writing, see Chapter 3.

Platforms and Nozzles

Whether or not your printer has a heated platform will determine what types of materials you can print. To determine what materials you want to print, consider the intended uses of your 3D prints. The first question is whether you want to create *functional* parts—parts that will be under some sort of load, like a motor mount on a robot.

Pretty much all the printers that use filament can print in polylactic acid (PLA), the biodegradable corn-based plastic we talk about in Chapter 2. However, PLA deforms at relatively low temperatures by plastic-melting standards (like that of a car dashboard in summer) and so is of limited use anyplace it will both be under load and warm. If a constant load is acting on it, it will deform slowly over time (known as *creeping*) even at room temperature. Many low-cost printers (and some pricier ones, too) are not designed to handle any materials other than PLA.

If your printers will mostly be used for small, decorative student projects like keychains, you should be able to stick with the simplicity of printing in PLA, which is by and large pretty forgiving to print with and relatively cheap. Figure 4-2 shows how good a PLA part can look—there are many different kinds now, and some have very good finishes.

Figure 4-2. *A PLA vase*

If you are making parts that have to withstand some banging around or do something useful, you will probably need a printer that can print in a wider range of materials. This in turn means that the printer needs to handle a bigger temperature range. For that, it will probably need to have an all-metal hot end (as opposed to one lined with polytetrafluoroethylene (PTFE), itself a plastic) and possibly a heated print bed. Some of these materials need to be used in an area that is ventilated well; see Chapter 5's discussion of ventilation. People often make parts that need to stand up to some repeated motion out of nylon, like Figure 4-3's extruder mount from a Bukito 3D printer (the white part).

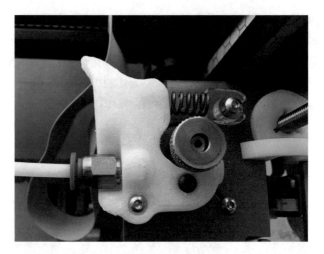

Figure 4-3. *Nylon functional part*

Note   Some filaments are very abrasive and will quickly wear out a nozzle. The "filled filaments," which consist of a PLA or other base polymer mixed with metal or composite materials like chopped carbon fiber, fall into this category, as do glow-in-the-dark filaments. Hardened steel or ruby-tipped replacement nozzles are intended to withstand abrasive filaments.

Some 3D printers can handle more exotic materials like polycarbonate, but these materials can require specialized hot ends, a platform that can be heated to a very high temperature, and a platform surface material that is compatible with the material being printed (see the discussion of materials in Chapter 2).

Higher-temperature materials tend to shrink as they cool if they are not kept continuously warm, hence the need for a heated platform. If the build platform is cold, each layer will shrink as it cools. The hot layer on top will misalign, and over time the corners of a print will warp and peel up from the platform. Having a heated platform mitigates this. There are exceptions. Nylon can be printed on a printer without a heated platform (the piece shown in Figure 4-3 was printed that way), but the platform material needs to be one that nylon will stick to, like Garolite LE.

An intermediate choice is polyethylene terephthalate glycol-modified (PETG), which can be printed on a printer without a heated bed. The material is usually a little more expensive than PLA, but tends to creep less than PLA. Figure 4-4 shows a hollow cube 20 mm on a side, printed in translucent PETG.

Figure 4-4. *Hollow cube printed in PETG*

So, the bottom line is: if you want to make 3D prints that do something mechanical, you are probably going to need a heated platform and an all-metal hot end. Table 4-1 summarizes this information. Note that you can use a heated bed with some of the materials listed here as not necessarily needing one, but you will need to use a platform surface other than blue painter's tape, because that tape's adhesive cannot handle heated bed temperatures.

Tip   There are a few published papers and dissertations on the strength of 3D printed ABS and PLA parts. They have found rather inconsistent results. Joshua Pearce's lab at Michigan Technical University has done some systematic studies in this sphere—for example, a paper by Nagendra G. Tanikella, Ben Wittbrodt, and Joshua M. Pearce: "Tensile Strength of Commercial Polymer Materials for Fused Filament Fabrication 3-D Printing." *Additive Manufacturing* 15: pp. 40–47 (2017). DOI: 10.1016/j.addma.2017.03.005.

Table 4-1. *Material Effects on Printer Requirements*

Material	Heated Bed Required?	Platform Surface	Nozzle
PLA	No	Blue tape	PTFE-lined or all-metal
ABS	Yes	PEI, PET tape, glue	All-metal
Nylon	No	Garolite LE	All-metal
PETG	No	Blue tape	All-metal
Filled PLA	No	Blue tape	Requires hardened nozzle

Multiple Extruders

Some printers come with two extruders. The purpose of the second one is to let you create prints with two colors or two materials. The best reason to use one of these is to use dissolvable support material. As we discuss in Chapter 2, because prints are created a layer at a time on the platform, anything with a steep enough overhang will require support material. Support material on a single-extruder printer requires that you snap off the material with pliers or other tools.

Dissolvable support is one solution to this, although the material tends to clog nozzles, and when you dissolve it you then need to get rid of the water with the dissolved material. Polyvinyl alcohol (PVA), the commonest material, is a relative of Elmer's glue, and it is not a great idea to put much Elmer's glue into your plumbing (and might not be legal). Talk to your waste-management person before creating a lot of gluey water.

High-impact polystyrene (HIPS) is another material used for dissolvable support. It dissolves in limonene, a cleaning solvent made from oranges. Here too you will need to check on local restrictions on getting rid of solvents. See Chapter 2 for more about materials, including these.

Caution   A two-extruder printer will not use both extruders to print something in half the time, although a few two-extruder printers have a limited ability to print two copies of the same object at once, and some offer more ambitious experimentation. Typically, printers will print a lot more slowly in two-material mode because they have to pause on each layer and execute commands to wipe off each nozzle so that it does not drool onto the print while the other extruder is laying down material. In other words, do not buy a dual-extruder printer thinking you will print two objects in parallel. There is no way to do that with printers on the market as of this writing, because you might bang into one object with the opposite extruder.

There are new systems appearing that will analyze your model and in effect print in two colors from one nozzle. As of this writing, they are still a little experimental for most consumer use but are something to watch in the future.

One Big Printer or Several Small Ones?

Libraries and schools often have the impulse to buy the biggest printer their budget will allow. However, 3D prints take a long time. If you have three small printers, they can all be chugging away creating different projects. If you only have one, then you will have a queue.

You can print more than one thing at a time on a print bed, but that has its own issues. First, you need to start them all at once. Second, if one print out of five on the bed has an issue that makes it fall off or fall over, most likely you will need to stop the entire print. It is usually better to have beginner prints run in isolation, one per printer, so that you can kill a print that has problems and send the student back to the drawing board.

Except in the case of tall, thin prints that would require extra cooling time, usually not much time is saved when you try to print multiple things on the same printer plate rather than print one after the other. These longer-running prints are more prone to failure. So this, too, argues that spreading prints across several small printers is often a better idea than plating them all at once on a big printer.

Small printers are easier to move around. Although it is not a good idea to move a printer if you can help it, if you are going to move it much you are better off with something that is, well, moveable. On the flip side, if you are concerned about theft (in a library public room, for example), a big printer is harder to steal, but also more awkward to move and lock up in a closet when a room is unattended. We have run a bicycle cable lock through the metal handle of our portable printer when we needed to leave it unattended at a show, but obviously you need to be sure any locking mechanism does not get in the way when the printer is moving.

There are exceptions, but by and large smaller printers are faster than bigger ones if they are printing something that will fit on either printer. 3D printers have to move the build platform and/or a carriage that is big enough to get to all parts of the print. Whipping around bigger carriages and platforms makes precise movement more challenging, and often you can print at better resolution in less time on a smaller printer. Smaller frames can also be stiffer, with similar positive results.

There are a few special cases when it is nice to have a bigger printer. Obviously, if you want to print something substantial frequently, and you think it would be a bad idea to glue several smaller pieces together, you may want a bigger printer.

Also, if you often print tall, skinny things, remember that printers can only put down material for a new layer when the previous one has cooled enough to hold its shape. This does not take very long, but tall, skinny prints will be limited by this minimum layer time. For these, it may take the same amount of time to print two or three things as it does to print just one (and the quality may be better, since the plastic cools better if the hot nozzle does not remain in contact with it). Of course, if something is tall and skinny, you can probably fit a few on your small print bed, as long as the print area is big enough.

We usually recommend buying a few small printers rather than one large one, unless there is a specific use case that requires a large printer.

Printer Connectivity

In Chapter 3, we talk about the types of software involved in using a 3D printer. Regardless of the printer, one way or another a set of commands to print a model has to get to the printer from a computer somewhere. Printers handle that in one of several ways: they require a USB cable to be connected to the computer that created the file of commands; they accept those commands wirelessly; or they read a file off an SD card or USB flash drive. Depending on your environment, each one of these has advantages.

Printers that require a hard USB connection the entire time they are running are somewhat unusual now. That is a disadvantage, because if the computer sleeps or is otherwise interrupted, the print can fail (not to mention that it ties up a computer). One way around this is to use Octoprint on a Raspberry Pi to control your printer (see Chapter 3's discussion of Octoprint). A MatterControl tablet (also in Chapter 3) will work as well.

Printers that receive files over wifi work well if you are in a stable wifi environment, but obviously it causes problems if you are not. We are partial ourselves to printers that hold their models on SD cards or other outside storage, since this works everywhere and does not tie up a computer. However, SD cards are small and easily misplaced. Printers often have an LCD screen to choose among the files on an SD card or files transmitted wirelessly.

Open Source Materials vs. Cartridges

Some printer manufacturers require (or at least encourage) you to use their proprietary materials. In some cases, a computer chip in the cartridge will take care of software settings for you automatically. The catch is that these materials will be vastly more expensive than their generic equivalents— sometimes three to five times more expensive. It also may mean you will not be able to try new materials that come along.

Particularly if you are in a cost-conscious environment, it is best to avoid being locked in to one manufacturer for your raw material. If nothing else, if your manufacturer goes out of business or stops supporting your printer, you will not be stuck if you can use open source materials.

That said, if you use generic (often called *open* or *open source*) filament, read reviews on Amazon and other popular retail websites. Very cheap filament sometimes has impurities that clog printers, or varies in diameter enough that it can cause printers to jam. Low-cost printers have in a way outsourced their precision to their filament, and if it varies more than a few percent in diameter or composition, you may not be able to use it at all. People become very brand loyal after a time. If you are starting out, you might consider getting recommendations for one or two brands and buy a small amount to be sure that it works well for your printer before stocking up.

Filament Size

Printer filament comes in two standard diameters: 1.75 mm and what is called (for historical reasons) "3 mm" filament but is usually close to 2.85. When you first buy your printer, you will typically buy two or three spools of filament with it. Over time, you will want to try a different color or material, and you will build up a pile of partial spools. It gets very irritating to have a mix of the two kinds, both because of the double storage space and, if you are moving your printers around, the possibility that the filament spool and printer will not match. As of this writing, Lulzbot and Ultimaker were the major manufacturers using 3 mm filament; most others use 1.75.

Tip   Filament should be kept in its original sealed package until first use, and then if at all possible in an airtight container to keep out moisture. Materials that absorb moisture (especially PVA, polycarbonate, and nylon) will tend to outgas and pop when heated, which can make pits in the print or jam the extruder and can weaken the prints. Five-gallon buckets with tight lids are a common solution. Resist the temptation to open and display every colorful spool as it arrives, unless you are in an extremely dry climate.

Enclosed or Open

Some 3D printers have open gantries (like a miniature construction crane), whereas others are completely sealed boxes. If you are printing acrylonitrile butadiene styrene (ABS), there are advantages to an enclosed box to keep the temperature more even. If young kids are around, a closed box will keep their hands away. An enclosure limits the visibility into what is going on, of course. This decision is closely related to the issue of where you are going to put it, discussed in Chapter 5. Some printers also have the option of built-in air filtration, which only makes sense with a closed printer.

Buy Within a Brand

If you are starting out and supplying a new makerspace, you may be tempted to try out several different brands of 3D printer. We recommend against that, because every 3D printer has quirks. If you stick to a particular brand, you will be able to learn and anticipate the issues a little better. It may also make training staff or students a little easier.

Should You Buy a Kit?

A lot of printers still come as kits. If you are confident in your ability to put together an electronic device, building a kit is a good way to really know how the printer works. However, if you have not tried anything like this before, and if there are no hackerspaces around that could help you, it might not be a good idea. Sometimes a high school robotics team is the early adopter and buys the first printer. If coaches and students are up for it, it might be a good off-season project.

Initial Costs, Filament Printing

We are often asked, "What will it cost for us to start a 3D printing lab?" As with everything to do with 3D printing, the answer is that it depends on what you are doing. If you want to buy, say, two small printers and one bigger one and run five to ten smallish projects a day, the cost of just the equipment breaks down something like this:

- *Smaller printers*: $500–$1000 each
- *Bigger printer*: $1500–$2500 each

- *Tools*: Initial purchase of incidental tools such as pliers, spatulas, tape, and glue: $200

- *Filament*: 4–8 kg PLA per month at $30/kg, or $120-$240/month

- *Miscellaneous supplies*: $20/month

Some printer manufacturers provide support contracts but most assume you will be on your own. Chapter 5 talks about living with your 3D printer and discusses facilities, ongoing costs such as training and maintenance, and similar staffing issues that affect lifecycle costs.

Selecting a Resin Printer

Resin printers can be divided into two major categories. The original technology, stereolithography (SLA), is less common today but is still used by some of the most popular manufacturers, including Formlabs. SLA printers use a laser galvanometer to draw out each layer in toolpaths that resemble those used by filament-based printers, though with a smaller spot size and moving much more quickly.

Most newer designs adapt technology used by visual display systems to expose a layer. This usually involves using a Digital Light Processing (DLP) projector, though in an effort to get the price down, some newer designs are using liquid-crystal display (LCD) masking to selectively illuminate the resin. In either case, the light intensity is much lower than with a laser, but these technologies have the advantage that they can illuminate an entire layer at once. The terminology of resin printers is in flux and is used somewhat inconsistently in the marketplace.

Some DLP printers have a built-in projector, and sometimes you have to provide an external one. If you see a suspiciously cheap DLP printer, you probably will have to buy a projector, too. These printers are coming down in price, but are still expensive to purchase and to run relative to filament printers.

Fundamentally, resin printers use a source of light to harden a light-sensitive resin. Some sort of solvent has to be used when the print comes out of the printer to wash off excess resin. The operational tradeoff comes down to whether you have a space that can handle a device that is more at home in a chemistry lab than a computer lab. Of course, if you have a chemistry lab, that is a pretty good place to keep it.

Caution   There have been many new resin printers on crowdfunding sites and exhibiting at maker events. They often use a cell phone as a source of light. Although this makes the "printer" incredibly cheap, there are several fundamental issues. First, your phone will be tied up for many hours for the print. Second, if you get a call or text, it will probably ruin the print. Finally, we will just say that we would not want to put one of our phones under a vat of resin that will harden when exposed to light from the phone.

Cleaning and Curing

Resin prints require cleaning and curing. *Cleaning* usually means washing them off with alcohol, which leaves you with a solution of alcohol and dissolved resin to dispose of. *Curing* can mean putting the prints out in the sun or exposing them to some source of UV light.

The resin in the vat must be kept extremely clean. Any stray bits of cured resin floating around can damage a print in progress or even the printer itself.

DLP vs. SLA

DLP printers, as discussed in Chapter 2, illuminate an entire layer at a time and can generate very fine detail. SLA printers move a laser spot. DLP theoretically can produce smaller features but will also show pixelation artifacts in all directions. SLA printers, on the other hand, should show smoother outlines within a layer but have a minimum spot size bigger than a DLP pixel. Relative speed of the technologies depends more on brand and the formulation of the resin being used than on the difference between the technologies. The technique used to peel each layer off the base of the vat makes an even bigger difference.

Proprietary Resins

As with filament printers, there are printers that require you to buy a proprietary resin (or at least highly encourage it) and there are those that allow you to use some types of generic resin. However, the tradeoffs are a little different here. One advantage of resin printing is the materials—it can create dental and other specialized parts, for example.

If you want to do something that requires a specialty material, you might want a printer that uses resin cartridges that communicate with the printer to optimize its settings. Resins optimized for metal casting exist, too, for jewelry making. But if you do not have a specialized technical objective in mind, you may want to buy a printer that can use generic resins.

Initial Costs, Resin Printing

Resin printing costs are pretty variable right now, but for rough comparison with our earlier estimates for filament printers (assuming several printers, averaging about 10 small prints per day), here are some rough numbers as of this writing (in early 2018):

- *SLA system*: $1300–$5000 each

- *DLP system (with integrated projector)*: $1400–$5000 each

- *Resin*: 4–8 liters per month at $60–$150/liter

- *Drying/cleaning devices*: Not essential but might save solvent and other materials—around $1000

- *Replacement trays/vats*: Replace every 5–10 liters for low end, more than that for higher end: $50–$100 each

- *Solvents (IPA, most commonly)*: Varies—consider disposal costs in your jurisdiction.

Using a Service Bureau Instead

If you want to let your students design objects to 3D print but all these choices sound overwhelming, you can always use a service bureau. That will be far more expensive, of course, than printing yourself. You may be hesitant to pay for printing a student project.

The cheapest bureau is likely to be a shared service, where people who have printers bid on jobs. Two of the big ones are www.3dhubs.com and www.makexyz.com. But even the lowest-cost one will charge many times the materials cost you would have if you did prints yourself. The way it works is that you post an STL file, and a service provider fulfills it—sort of like Uber for 3D printers. It will be a mix of bigger and smaller vendors.

You may want to have some small test part printed as a data point to see the cost, quality, and turnaround time. Remember, though, that many of these providers are one-person shops with a few printers (and may even be a teenager), so if you throw a whole school at them, they may not be the ones who end up handling a sudden large order.

Summary

This chapter discussed some of the major hardware choices that you have to make in selecting a 3D printer, particularly a filament-using one. We went over the different types of materials you might want to use to create objects and the requirements for common filament types. We also gave some rough estimates of startup costs. In the next chapter, we talk about what happens once your printers arrive, and what the facilities and staff issues might be.

CHAPTER 5

Living with Your 3D Printer

In Chapter 4, we talk about how to buy a 3D printer. In this chapter, we discuss what to anticipate when you bring it into its new home and unpack it. You do not need an expensive, special space for it, but knowing a few things about what a 3D printer really does *not* like might save you a lot of grief.

We cover what physical space makes a printer less prone to fail, what it takes to train typical non-technical staff users, and maintenance requirements. In this chapter, we also talk you through how to create and print a small cube, a 3D printing equivalent of printing "hello world" when learning a new programming language.

Note The bulk of this chapter focuses on filament-based printers, which are far more common in the school and library environment. We have a short section at the end of this chapter summarizing the issues for a resin printer.

© Joan Horvath, Rich Cameron 2018
J. Horvath and R. Cameron, *Mastering 3D Printing in the Classroom, Library, and Lab*,
https://doi.org/10.1007/978-1-4842-3501-0_5

Getting Started with a Filament Printer

When you look at many consumer-level filament-based 3D printers, it is easy to forget that you are looking at a little precision factory. The temperature, airflow, vibration environment, and ambient dust in the room all matter to the quality of your print (and to the lifetime of your printer).

Bigger, enclosed printers are less vulnerable to some of these things, but for the price of one of those you may be able to get several smaller ones that can live tucked into suitable corners. In this chapter, we give you some background you can use to trade off those costs.

Where to Put It

Very often, people do not ask this question until the box arrives. Filament-based 3D printers should be in a room as free of dust as possible. Yet you want them in a ventilated area (particularly if you plan to use ABS). We will go through some of the common options here and talk about pluses and minuses.

A first impulse with a 3D printer in an educational environment is to think about making up a nice cart with the printers on top and the filament spools in the bottom part. However, doing this has many issues:

- 3D prints take a long time. Typical print times will range from an hour or two to several days. Most consumer printers cannot be reliably stopped and restarted, but features that allow a printer to recover from a power failure (with varying degrees of reliability) are becoming more common. Without this ability, you cannot unplug it and move it while printing, and even for printers that do have the capability, it is not intended to be used routinely (and will likely leave a visible artifact in the print).

- Carts are wobbly and often pretty flimsy, and do not provide a very stable base for the printer. You might have to recalibrate the printer every time you move around if you are jouncing over thresholds and other obstacles when you move the cart.

- If you have more than one printer running on a cart, that can end badly if they move around and you neglect to check that they are clear of each other for the whole range of their motion.

- Carts can get jounced around during a print, also causing artifacts.

- Filament needs to be protected from heat and moisture, which can be hard to do consistently rolling around on a cart.

- It can be challenging to think through ventilation issues if the cart will be going many arbitrary places.

In our experience, 3D printers that start off moving on a cart fairly quickly wind up in a permanent home instead. Or the cart gets tucked solidly in some corner and never moved, which defeats the purpose.

Tip   Although it is good for students to see their creations being made, one option is to do some short in-class demonstration prints and then print from an SD card, cloud storage, or whatever your printer supports thereafter. A science room or art room that students pass through on some regular basis can be a home for printers, if there is no "maker space" per se.

That then brings us back to the question: where should I put it? For most printers, a sturdy table or shelf in a reasonably clean room with good ventilation is the best bet. A printer should never be in direct sunlight, and all printers should not be too close to a heat vent or area that gets very hot when the air conditioning is off. One particular early printer of our acquaintance (that had 3D printed parts) turned into a Dali version of itself when left in a sunny window with the air conditioner off on a particularly hot summer weekend.

Caution   If you do have to move a printer frequently, be sure you are picking it up by its frame and not it up by one of its precision parts, like one of the axes, or (worse) by a belt. Printers intended to be portable sometimes have a handle. If yours does not, stop and think about whether you might be bending or otherwise putting unusual stress on a critical part when you pick it up.

Ventilation and Drafts

3D printers are melting plastic, which means it is always prudent to make sure you have adequate ventilation. If you are printing ABS or one of the more exotic filaments in particular, it is wise to have active ventilation (a fan) pulling air away from the printer. A lab or art space that is designed with similar issues in mind can be a good home for a printer for those reasons as well. Some spaces use freestanding filters in addition, and some printers come enclosed with filtration.

One person's "ventilation" can be another's "draft." Drafts can either be a plus or minus, depending on the material. Air flowing across the printer may make the bed struggle to maintain temperature, particularly if the ambient air is chilly. The exception to this is that having a fan blowing on a PLA print can improve print quality, particularly if you are printing on blue tape at ambient temperature (and thus not affecting heated bed temperature).

There are aftermarket "safety enclosures" for some printers that you can consider, and filtration is available for some enclosed printers.

Noise

3D printers vary widely in how much noise they make when running. Your best bet is to see if you can be around whatever one you are going to buy to assess whether it can live in a particular room without bothering the occupants. On the other hand, a 3D printer wants to live in a reasonably low-vibration environment, so you probably do not want to banish it to a loading dock either.

In noisy trade show environments, it is often difficult to hear the noise a printer makes at all. The same printer may be annoyingly loud in an otherwise silent room. Some tables, lightweight wooden ones in particular, may resonate in a way that more than doubles the apparent volume of the noise the printer makes. If your printer sounds significantly quieter when lifted just above the table while printing, you might want to consider special vibration-dampening feet or other means of isolating the printer from the table.

Dust

3D printers are precision machines. Nozzles on filament machines are typically less than half a millimeter in diameter, and it does not take much to clog them. For a filament printer, the little kludge in Figure 5-1 works quite well. Take a piece of microfiber fabric (like a Swiffer) or just a paper towel, and binder-clip it loosely onto the filament ahead of the extruder gear so that the filament slides freely through it. Be sure it is well clear of any moving part. Swap it out once in a while and judge whether or not it is necessary by how dirty it is when you take it off.

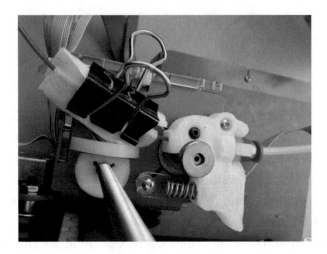

Figure 5-1. *A DIY dust catcher*

If you search on "filament cleaner" you will get other gadgets and folklore on ways to deal with this issue. Some of these advise using a cotton ball or sponge, but a cotton ball can be a source of particles that will cause an even worse clog. Sponges can dry out and lose contact with the filament. We do not recommend either of these methods.

There are also aftermarket enclosures and covers that you can buy to manage these issues. Joan leaves an upside-down large fabric shopping bag (handles down) over her open-frame printer if she is not going to use it for a while.

If, despite all your best efforts, your nozzle clogs, see the section on unclogging a nozzle later in this chapter.

Caution   Do not have 3D printer in a room with woodworking, pottery, or other activities that create fine dust.

Storing Filament

Filament should be stored in a cool, dry place without big temperature swings. Keep them in their original packaging until you are ready to use them. Consumer 3D printers have in some ways outsourced their precision to their filament manufacturers. Filament can absorb water from the air, and this is a bigger problem for some materials than others. For ones that absorb it very easily (notably nylon and PVA), the water will pop and boil off when the filament is heated, which can cause pitting on the surface and poor layer to layer adhesion.

If you live in a humid climate, keep your filament tightly sealed in a plastic bag with desiccant when you are not using it. Avoid leaving your printer and filament outside overnight or allowing water to condense on them. There are also filament-drying devices, but because we live in a mostly arid climate, we have not tried them personally.

PLA filament is the most forgiving of conditions except excessive heat. Do not leave a spool of PLA filament in a hot car on a summer day. Other than that, most reasonably sealed filament will be useable for years.

Tip   Tightly sealed 5-gallon paint containers work well to keep several rolls of filament sealed up. Stacking plastic boxes with tight lids work well too. You can place a renewable dehumidifier in the container with filament to keep its environment dry. These plastic modules contain a desiccant and a heating element that you can use by plugging it in once it has been saturated to remove the absorbed moisture from it.

Your First Print

In Chapter 3, we discuss all the many and varied software settings that come up in the general case of creating a 3D print. Here we give you a short summary of how to print something to get started. Resist the beginner temptation to download something complicated for your first print. Instead, create a small cube. The classic test cube is 20 mm on a side—a little under an inch. (3D printing is a metric world.)

The simplest way to do that is to use the free software package Tinkercad (`www.tinkercad.com`.) Tinkercad is web-based and recommends using a Chrome browser, or Firefox in a pinch. You will need to set up an Autodesk account. Then open Tinkercad. It has tutorials, but if you just want to make a simple cube, click Create New Design and drag the cube from the menu of shapes on the side to the workplane.

The default cube is, as it happens, 20 mm on a side. You do not have to do anything now except save the file. Figure 5-2 is a picture of a 20 mm 3D printed cube, with the bottom of the cube in the foreground so that you can see the pattern on the bottom as well as the layers. A happy print should look like this—nice clean bottom layer, and regular layering up from it.

Figure 5-2. A 20 mm cube

To save it, click Export ➤ Download for 3D Printing. You should now have a file with a name ending in .stl.

The next step is to load this STL file into software that will turn this model into commands for your printer, usually called a *host program* or *slicing software*. Hopefully your manufacturer pointed you to either its own program or one of the open source free options. If not, MatterControl (`www.mattercontrol.com`), Ultimaker Cura 3 (`https://software.ultimaker.com`), and Slic3r (`www.slic3r.org`) are all commonly used. Chapter 3 details how to use these programs to create a file that can control your printer, called a *G-code file* on most printers (but a proprietary format on others).

Calibrating Your Printer

A critical requirement for good 3D prints is having the printer's parts align correctly *to each other*. This requires that the printer be both *square* and *tram*. *Squaring* refers to ensuring that the axes are at right angles to one another, whereas *tram* and *tramming* are used specifically to refer to adjustment of the *build platform* to ensure that it is parallel to the *x*/*y* motion of the machine.

A 3D printer that is square but not tram will have the axes at right angles, but the nozzle will not maintain the same distance from the platform as the *x* and *y* axes move. A machine that is tram but not square will usually print fine, but the angles will be wrong so that rectangles will become parallelograms and circles will become ovals.

If you suspect that your machine's axes are out of alignment because prints that should be rectangles are skewed, first check that the axes are square relative to each other (use a carpenter's square or, in a pinch, any other stiff, accurate rectangular object). If they are not, use whatever adjustments your printer manufacturer provides.

Depending on how your printer is constructed, this may require loosening several screws, nudging parts into alignment, and retightening the screws to lock them in place. Other designs may make this more difficult if the misalignment is due to bad manufacturing tolerances. These issues can be more difficult to fix, but can often be solved with strategic use of shims. If the error is in a part that can be printed and you feel competent to modify your printer, consider making a new one without the error as a more permanent fix (but save the old one, just in case).

If the width of an extruded line is inconsistent from one end of the platform to the other, check the alignment of the build platform relative to the axes, hereafter referred to as *tramming the platform*. Always check your squareness first, though, because if you have to make any adjustment your frame, you will need to tram the platform all over again.

Caution   Some manufacturers refer to "leveling" a platform, but we try to avoid this terminology because it often leads to confusion about how to go about dealing with a platform that is not "level." Do *not* use a bubble level to align your platform. If you have your printer on a table that is not level, but your printer is otherwise square, changing any printer adjustment based on a bubble level would most likely not fix the problem. We use the word *tram* to draw this distinction about internally consistent alignment of the printer axes relative to the platform versus level relative to gravity. Note that the axes are imaginary lines in space; normally, the printer's linear motion components will be lined up with the axes, but in principle software can compensate if they are not. Be sure you understand what your printer does and does not compensate for before attempting to fix problems.

If the build platform gets out of tram, either you can wind up printing in air in places where the platform is lower than expected or mashing the first few layers on parts of the platform that are too close to the nozzle. Prints that do not stick in one corner and are a bit mashed (with wider-than-normal extrusion lines) on another part of the platform are symptoms of this problem.

A typical way to fix this for most printers is to home the axes manually (see the section "Manually Controlling Your Printer" in Chapter 3). Then take a piece of paper (we like to use a sticky note by sticking it to our fingers and placing it sticky-side-up on the platform) and move your extruder in x and y near each of the adjustment screws for your platform. For most printers, the piece of paper should be able to get between the platform and the nozzle, but there should be a bit of resistance. There is a device called a *feeler gauge* that does the same thing, but do not use one—a feeler gauge is made of a metal that is harder than your nozzle and might damage it.

As a quick test, you can print a small item with a big skirt (a skirt that is near the edges of the platform) to check platform tram. If the skirt does not lay down evenly, then you need to try again.

Some machines have "auto-leveling" features. These features use some kind of sensor to probe the height of the platform in various locations to ascertain how it is (mis)aligned and then apply a transformation matrix in software to align the printer's coordinate system to the platform, rather than vice versa. This can make it a lot easier for a beginner to set up a printer, but it is better not to rely on these features if you can avoid it. In some cases, rounding errors in these calculations can cause unsightly lines in the surfaces of prints, especially if your logical axes end up very close to, but not quite perfectly aligned to, the physical axes of a Cartesian printer. This is less of an issue for non-Cartesian printers, because their physical axes are not straight and they are already doing similar math to translate Cartesian coordinates.

When a Print Starts

When you have successfully sliced a part to create G-code and used a host program to send it to the printer (both of which are described in Chapter 3), what happens next depends on what is in the G-code, and also on the printer's firmware. If your manufacturer gave you standard settings files, it is likely that there are some G-codes that are added to the beginning of every print to *home* one or more of the axes (to bring the nozzle to some known point relative to the platform). Homing involves moving the extruder to a predetermined starting point, usually with each of the printer's physical axes at one of its two extremes, and touching a switch or triggering some other feedback mechanism to let the controller know that it is there. Aside from homing, most printers run their axes open-loop, moving the motors in discrete steps and counting steps to determine their location relative to home. The printer will also need to wait for the extruder and the platform heater (if there is one) to reach the specified temperature(s), and may do this before or after homing, depending on the order of commands in the start code.

Once the extruder and platform reach the right temperature, the extruder will usually drool a little to get some filament melted before the print proper starts. Then the printer will start to print a skirt (if you specified one) and then your print.

The first time you see a 3D printer making an object, it is mesmerizing. There is an in-joke in the community that the second item people print out is a chin rest so that they can watch their prints in comfort.

Tip   Slicing programs give estimates of build times, but the actual build times may vary. This is because the firmware does not move at exactly the speeds specified in the G-code, but rather accelerates and decelerates each time it changes direction, making its average speed lower. These calculations occur in the firmware, so the host program does not know how much this will affect the print time; some hosts offer better estimates than others.

During a Print

Once a print starts successfully, there is not a lot to do except to keep an eye on it in case something goes wrong. It is not a good idea to leave a 3D printer unattended, just as you would not go too far from a turned-on stove or oven. After a while, you will be able to tell from the sounds your printer makes if all is well. 3D prints can take a long time (many hours is common), and in the beginning we recommend small tests of new techniques and materials so you can watch the proceedings actively and intervene if the print does not go as planned.

The commonest failure is having the print come loose and slosh around. The only thing to do in that case is to kill the job (from the host program, or by resetting the printer) and change some of the design to have a bigger footprint on the build platform, or perhaps print at a bit higher temperature. If a print just does not look right, go back to Chapter 3 and consider changing some of the slicing settings; look at Chapter 2 to see if the filament properties might be the problem; and consider troubleshooting ideas in this chapter if you suspect your printer. The platform may not have been adequately aligned and prepared.

When a Print Finishes Normally

When your part finishes printing, ideally the result will be a part sitting on the build platform looking just like you imagined it would. However, you still need to get the piece off the platform without breaking it. How do you get any support, brims, and so on off the part? And what should you do to be sure the printer is ready either to be turned off for the day or to print the next job?

Caution   If your printer has a heated build platform, wait for it to cool down somewhat before you remove the part. Otherwise, the part (which is still a little soft) may bend or warp as you take it off or if it cools too quickly off the platform.

Getting a Part off the Build Platform

Once the print has cooled down (see the preceding Caution), sometimes you can just grasp a part firmly and snap it off the platform. Depending on the combination of platform surface and print material you use, you may find that a print releases almost on its own as the platform cools. Usually, though, you need a little leverage to get it started. You may also find that there is some intermediate temperature at which the print is easier to pry loose, but that it is more difficult once the print and platform have fully cooled. Keeping a part firmly attached while printing but allowing it to be easily removed afterward is one of the more difficult issues in 3D printing. If a print breaks loose too early, it can ruin a print, but sometimes the pieces adhere a little too well.

Unless your manufacturer recommends another implement, a common tool to pry pieces off the build platform is one of the tools used by artists: a paint knife (shown in Figure 5-3), an artist's spatula, or a palette knife. These work well on blue and Kapton tape. Get one that is fairly stiff so that it is strong enough to move a substantial part. The exact form factor is a matter of taste and experience, but the shape in Figure 5-3 works well.

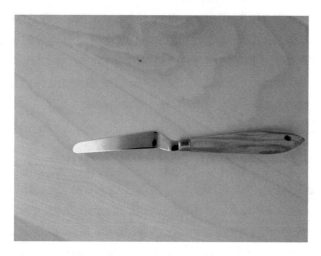

Figure 5-3. *A painting knife is a good tool to remove a part from a tape-covered platform*

Any art supply house should carry these tools (for example, Blick's, at www.dickblick.com). Very sharp edges should not be necessary, and you particularly want to avoid sharp corners like those of a razor blade that will scrape your platform, as these can damage the surface and force you to replace it more often. Once you get your tool under a corner, try twisting it to lift that corner rather than sliding the tool further under where it may scrape the platform surface.

While we are talking about small, handy tools to have in your kit, you should also get a good pair of tweezers, which are useful for plucking bits of drooled filament out of places they should not be.

Picking Off Support and Cleaning Up the Print

If your part needed support, you now have to pick it off. This can be a painstaking process, and the precise procedure you use will depend on the shape of your print and the tools you have available. Be careful because the plastic can be sharp; protect your eyes with safety glasses from the possibility of small, flying, sharp bits.

Grasping the support with needle-nosed pliers and twisting it sometimes works well for sparse support; experiment and see what works for you. As discussed in Chapter 6, it is best to design your model in the first place to avoid big areas of support because they are very hard to remove. Chapter 8 discusses finishing techniques.

Restarting or Shutting Off the Printer

When you take your print off the build platform, you can either turn off the printer or create your next print. If your manufacturer gave you slicing settings, it is likely that there are some shutdown lines of G-code in the standard setting, or the firmware may take care of some activities.

For example, a printer without a heated build platform might add a few lines to every G-code file like those in the following example. The first line turns off the extruder heater (sets the temperature to zero); the second line sends the x-axis to its home (zero) position; and the last command disables all motors:

```
M104 S0
G28 X0
M84
```

In general, if a print finished normally, you probably can create or load in another G-code and just run the next job. If you are not planning on using the printer again right away, it is best to turn it off and possibly unplug it.

Manually Controlling Your Printer

From time to time, you may suspect that your printer has a problem, or you may need to manually back out of an awkward failure that left a part skewered on the extruder. In those cases, you will want to use the Print or Control window in one of the host programs to send a G-code single line or two, or use the other manual controls that most host programs provide.

There are measures you may want to take as part of routine printing. For example, what do you do if you want to change filament colors, but you forgot to pull out the previous filament when you turned off the printer (and now it has cooled down and gotten stuck in the nozzle)?

Note   Some printers allow you to perform some or all of the functions we describe here from an LCD interface on the printer rather than in software as we describe here. Check your manufacturer's directions for the precise steps to take to solve these common issues.

All the procedures that follow use the printer control mode in the host program you are using, as described in Chapter 3's discussion of host programs. There are variations among the hosting programs, but all of them allow sending a single line of G-code at a time, as well as moving the extruder in any axis, heating the extruder, and heating the platform.

Tip   By default, most printers use degrees Celsius (C) for temperature and millimeters (mm) for length measurements. If you are having trouble thinking in metric, keep in mind that there are exactly 25.4 mm in an inch, 210 degrees C equals 410 Fahrenheit, 115 C is 239 F, and 230 C is 446 F (to pick some commonly encountered temperatures).

Stopping a Print

Sometimes a print does not stick to the platform and starts to slosh around, or the print you thought would be fine without support is not going to work after all, or you just look at what is building and scratch your head about how your lovely computer image could have turned out like that. When a problem like this becomes obvious, the best thing to do is to click the "Kill Job" or "Stop" button, as the case may be in your host program.

If the print got jammed under the extruder somehow, you may want to move the extruder away manually (see "Backing Out of a Bad Situation" later in this chapter) and then retract the filament. Once you get the failed print off the build platform, turn off the printer if you are not going to try again. Note that G-code to turn off heaters and other shutdown activities will not be executed if the job was killed partway through. Your host program's stop function may shut down the heaters for you, but probably will not do any of those other things.

Typically, it is a good idea to cycle (turn off, wait, then turn back on) power to the printer just in case the partial print left it in some strange mode. If the failure rammed anything into the extruder, you might want to check that the build platform was not thrown out of alignment. Check your manufacturer's alignment instructions.

Changing Filament

When you finish printing a part, it is a good practice to retract the filament out of the nozzle before it cools completely, so that you will not have to heat it up again to remove it if you want to print with a different one next time. To retract the filament, as soon as the print job finishes, open the printer control panel and type in 10 mm of retraction. You can click the button to extrude 10 mm a few times; the filament should pop out of the input device after an appropriate number.

If you have a Bowden extruder (see Chapter 2), you only really need to get it out of the hot end to have the option of pulling it out easily later. Some printers also add commands to retract after every print job so you do not have to think about it. Even these printers, though, normally do not retract if you kill a job mid-print for some reason.

Suppose you forgot to retract the filament last time. You have bright pink ABS filament in the nozzle and you want to make an object in white in PLA. If your printer does not have a touchscreen option to facilitate this process, you will need to use one of the host programs described in Chapter 3. The steps will be something along these lines, with details dependent on which software package you elect to use:

- Type in the temperature appropriate to the *filament that is in the nozzle* (in this case, ABS, so about 230 degrees; see Chapter 2).

- Turn on the extruder heater (typically by clicking a button).

- Look at the monitoring display in the host software and wait until the temperature is near the right level (but not all the way there, because then you will just melt more filament into the nozzle).

- Retract 10 mm at a time until the filament springs out (or until you can pull it out the rest of the way, for printers that have a release).

- Then change the extruder temperature to the level appropriate *for the new filament* (in this case, PLA, so about 210 degrees). If there is plastic left in the nozzle, purge it by pushing it out with the new filament. This has to be done at the higher of the two extrusion temperatures (in this case, 230 C). If there is a big temperature difference between the two filaments, you may have to use an intermediate filament to purge out the old one, or use the "cold pull" technique described later in this chapter to clean it out.

- Start the new filament into the extruder in whatever way is appropriate for your printer once the extruder is at the appropriate temperature (look at the temperature status graph).

- Once it is nearly in, type in 40 mm or so and extrude.

- Keep extruding an additional 10 mm or so at a time until the filament stops coming out the old color. Using a skirt on your next print will take some of that away too.

- You can then run your next print with the new color and material.

Tip   You could, in principle, use the preceding process to change out filament mid-run to have a multi-color or multimaterial print with one extruder. Experts can and do try this (by using "pause"). It is very tricky, though, and results may be unpredictable.

Changing Temperatures During a Print

If a print looks like it may be having trouble sticking to a heated platform, you might want to raise the platform temperature just a few degrees. Your printer might have a way to do this through a touchscreen or other controls on the printer itself. Assuming you are not so lucky but that you have a computer connected while the printer is running, you will need to type a new temperature in a host program (but not a slicing program) under Heated bed. There will be a Set or similar button to click to confirm changing the settings. You can change your extrusion temperature on the fly this way too (by changing extruder temperature and clicking Set) if you decide you should be running a little hotter or cooler.

Basic Hardware Troubleshooting

Sometimes you will want to determine whether a printer is having hardware issues of some type, so it is good to be able to try some basic commands to debug what is going on.

Checking the Motion of One Axis at a Time

If you want to check the motion of one axis in a controlled fashion to see whether something is broken or loose, the printer control panel in the host programs (see Chapter 3) allows you to move the axis in a positive or negative direction by typing in a positive or negative number (or in some cases by clicking buttons with fixed positive and negative increments). In Chapter 2, you saw that the z-axis is the vertical axis; x and y are in the plane of the build platform.

If nothing happens when you enter a value, you may be at an end stop. Try entering a small value to move in the opposite direction. (For example, if nothing happens when you input -10 mm in x, then try +10 mm). Use small values—a few millimeters —if you are trying to debug a problem. Some machines are also configured with software endstops. It is not uncommon for machines to refuse to move in the negative direction past the point where they were when the machine started up until it has been homed, because it thinks that that position is zero.

If no axis will run, you may have a connection problem; be sure your USB connector is firmly attached and that your printer hardware settings are correct for your printer. Some printers may be able to power up their controllers and communicate with a host program using USB power, even if the printer's power supply is not plugged into the wall or its switch is off. Power to drive the motors and heaters can only come from the printer's power supply, though, so these functions will not work without it.

Backing Out of a Bad Situation

If you forget to take a previous print off the platform, or otherwise do something you are not supposed to do, you may find the extruder jammed into a print or blocked somehow. Because it is hard to figure out which way is +x and which way is –y under battle conditions, you might want to familiarize yourself now with how your printer is set up in case you need to walk your way out of a problem with the manual controls.

Extruder Not Extruding

If the extruder is moving around but no material is coming out, there are a few possible problems. The extruder nozzle might be jammed, or the extruder motor might not be pushing out filament. To debug this problem, you may have to trick the printer a little to get the information you need.

Most printers are set up so that the drive system does not try to push filament through a cold extruder. However, for printers with a visible filament drive gear, it is helpful to see whether the gears are turning even though nothing is coming out. A drive gear and its relationship to filament are shown in Figure 5-4. You may not be able to see anything if filament is stuck in the nozzle. But if no filament is in the extruder drive, you might be able to send an M302 G-code command to the printer to tell it to override the need to heat up the extruder. Then tell the gear to extrude a few tens of millimeters of filament. See if the gears are turning. If not, you have some other failure.

Figure 5-4. *A visible (Bowden extruder) filament drive gear*

If the gears do turn, then your nozzle is probably clogged. To unclog a nozzle, follow your manufacturer's instructions. If your manufacturer did not provide any suggestions, you can try the following:

- Heat the extruder a little above what you used for your last print and try manually extruding, as we did for the filament-changing process earlier this chapter. If you have input an M302 command, be careful not to try to extrude any filament until the head is at the appropriate temperature.

- If nothing comes out, manually retract the filament. Take a look at the end of it—is there anything burned or strange on it?

- If not, try breaking off the end cleanly and extruding again.

- If all that fails, try the "cold pull" procedure described in this chapter.

- You might also try searching online using the phrase "Unclog extruder *<your printer name here>*."

Clearing a Clogged Nozzle

One of the more common problems with a 3D printer is that the printer stops extruding plastic because the extruder nozzle is clogged. The nozzle hole is small and it can fairly easily be blocked with debris that was embedded in the filament, dust, or plastic that got too hot and scorched or burned.

Caution   If your nozzle is not rated to 240 degrees C, you should not try to use nylon for this procedure.

Cold Pull

In the past, the only way to get a clog out of a nozzle was to take the entire hot end (nozzle, barrel, and heater block) apart or take it off and put it in a solvent. Because that is not very convenient, and taking the hot end apart can damage it, the *cold-pull* technique was developed. Somewhere along the line it also developed the name *atomic pull*, but we call it by its older name here. A cold pull starts with inserting filament in the nozzle just as if you were going to print with the filament.

Instead of using the usual extrusion temperature, though, which would melt the filament, a cold pull involves pulling the plastic out at a lower temperature. The temperature is warm enough to allow the plastic to stretch enough to pull away from the sides of the barrel so that it does not seize up entirely, but cold enough so that the filament remains solid enough to stay in one piece. Usually, any debris in the nozzle will then come out with the filament. We estimate the best *cold-pull temperature* in the following description.

The cold-pull technique works best with printers that have polished-smooth stainless steel nozzle barrels. It also works for nozzles that have a polytetrafluoroethylene (PTFE) internal coating if they are rated to 240 C. The cold-pull technique has been successfully done with ABS (cold-pull temperature of about 160–180 C). PLA is much more difficult to work with, but a cold-pull temperature of 80–100 C will sometimes work. Nylon 618 filament (cold-pull temperature of 140 C) is far easier and more reliable to use for this purpose due to its strength, flexibility, and low friction.

The cold-pull technique works as follows: to begin, remove as much of the plastic that you've been using as possible. To do this, you can attempt a cold pull with ABS or PLA with the temperatures listed previously. For the rest of the instructions, we will assume that this failed to fully remove the filament.

Next, heat your nozzle to 240 C so that it can thoroughly melt the nylon and push the nylon filament in. If your printer has a Bowden tube, you may find it easier to remove it so that you can push and pull the filament by hand. Attempt to extrude the nylon slowly. Most clogs (especially those caused by accumulated dust) will not actually block the nozzle entirely, but will be pushed into the nozzle and stop it when the nozzle pressure increases and then float up out of the way when left to sit.

If you do not have a hard clog (usually a solid foreign particle lodged in the nozzle), a slow, pausing extrusion should allow you to purge the old printing material.

Once nylon starts coming out of the tip, you can begin cooling your nozzle. See Chapter 3 for information on manually controlling your printer to see how to extrude some filament by hand. You want to keep trying to push the filament slowly into the nozzle as it cools to prevent voids from plastic oozing out.

When your extruder temperature is well below the pull temperature, start heating it again to the specified temperature. When it gets close, start pulling on the filament manually if your printer mechanism allows it, or by retracting it using a host program (this requires the M302 command). Pulling as the temperature is rising allows you to ensure that it releases at the lowest possible temperature, which will make the filament more solid. Nylon should come out solid and nozzle-shaped, which is why it works best. Other materials often will not release until they are soft enough that they will stretch significantly. If this happens, you may still be able to get a successful pull if you are careful not to let the long, thin strand of plastic break.

Note   The temperatures specified in the preceding directions are maximum temperatures—temperatures above which the plastic is unlikely to come out solid. For best results, you should always pull the plastic at the lowest possible temperature.

Figure 5-5 shows some examples of cold pulls. If you pull the nylon out and the surface is rough, dark, discolored, or has black spots around the sides, this indicates that there is residue of overheated or carbonized, burned plastic in the nozzle. If you see this, you should clip off the end and repeat the process until the nylon comes out smooth, clean, and mostly white. Figure 5-6 shows similar examples from with a nozzle that was clogged with overheated plastic, rather than burned plastic.

Figure 5-5. *Burned residue on cold-pulled filament*

Tip   You might want to do cold pulls from time to time as a preventative measure if your print quality seems to be degrading.

Figure 5-6. *Nylon with residue of overheated plastic*

Dealing with a Hard Clog

Usually a cold pull can remove debris from a nozzle. However, if you cannot get the plastic all the way in to perform one, there is probably a hard bit of debris blocking your nozzle.

One solution is to pluck a bristle from a wire brush and push it into the nozzle using needle-nose pliers. Figures 5-7 and 5-8 show the process of pulling a bristle from a wire brush and pushing it into the nozzle. Once you have poked it through, try a cold pull to see if you can pull the debris out. Note that the nozzle has to be hot for this maneuver to work, because otherwise the nozzle will be clogged with solid plastic. Be careful not to get your fingers near the hot nozzle.

Using one of these tools does not usually remove the blockage from the nozzle entirely. It only dislodges the clog so that hot plastic can flow past it and then harden around it so that it can be pulled out, though occasionally it will break up the clog enough to allow it to be pushed out of the nozzle in smaller pieces.

Figure 5-7. *Extracting a single bristle from a wire brush*

Figure 5-8. *Using the wire brush bristle to clear out the nozzle*

Caution   Some sellers sell tiny drill bits for this purpose, but using these is a bad idea because they are brittle and are likely to break off in the nozzle, making your problem worse. Even if they work, their hard, sharp edges can scrape the softer brass of the nozzle (this is the same type of drill bit that was used to create that hole in the first place) and result in uneven extrusion.

Clicking or Grinding Noises

One of the first signs of trouble with a 3D printer is an unfamiliar noise. You will know you are an experienced 3D printer user when certain noises make you immediately execute a high-speed dive across the room toward your printer. Because prints can take many hours, listening to your printer is often the best way to monitor it (with an occasional glance, of course).

Tip   In addition to being sensitive to abnormal noises, be aware of what a "normal" print run smells like. A burning smell is never a good thing around electronics. Be able to distinguish problems from, say, the smell of ABS printing.

A filament-based printer has to drive the filament into the extruder somehow. Clicking noises usually means that the filament is not going into the nozzle smoothly (or at all). Here are some possible causes:

- The filament might be hung up on the spool or catching on something.

- The nozzle might be clogged, as just discussed.

- The filament might not have been seated correctly when it was inserted. (This applies at the beginning of a print; if the ticking starts mid-print, this is unlikely.)

- The filament might be too wide to go into the nozzle (check it with calipers as discussed in Chapter 2).

- Something might be hitting one of the fans on your printer. Check that the fans are clear.

- If your nozzle is too close to the platform, you may have trouble extruding in the early layers because the plastic coming out of the nozzle does not have anywhere to go.

Sudden grinding noises usually mean that the print came loose and is jammed under the nozzle. This warrants a sprint across the room to turn off the printer, because the jammed part can exert some unexpected forces on the platform and its supports. Get your printer into a safe condition by stopping the print job. Then manually walk the extruder back out using the techniques in the section "Backing Out of a Bad Situation." You may have to re-adjust the build platform as described earlier in this chapter.

Note   If you have been trying to extrude filament into a clogged nozzle, the drive gear may have been digging into the filament and clogging up the gears with ground-up filament. Check this too if you had to clear the nozzle. Otherwise, filament may not feed well, and you might think that the nozzle is still clogged. Pick and/or blow it off carefully and be sure you are not blowing plastic dust someplace where it will cause other problems.

Post-processing Tools and Space

Depending on what you are doing with your 3D prints, you may need some additional tools to use to clean up or otherwise post-process prints. In Chapter 8 we talk about artist studio considerations, which may require gluing, sanding, painting, and similar operations (and thus a facility that can handle those things). Earlier in this chapter we discuss printers needing to be in a clean environment; this may mean that you will want the post-processing to happen away from the printers.

Removing support can be a little messy and result in lots of small bits of plastic everywhere. Doing this over carpet is a bad idea since you will be picking the bits out forever. If the 3D printers are in a computer-lab type environment with carpets and nice tables, you may want to designate a "messy room" for the post-processing activities.

Chapters 8 through 12 address applications of 3D printers in various discipline situations. If you are outfitting a makerspace at a school or catering to teachers, you may want to skim through those chapters to get an idea of what types of materials you might want to keep in stock, beyond filament.

Recycling Prints

People ask us all the time if you can recycle your 3D prints into filament. Many people are working on that. The challenge, though, is that consumer 3D printing has, in a way, outsourced its precision to filament. If the filament diameter is off even a few hundredths of a millimeter, it can cause you problems. So, any local machine would need to produce very high quality and high volume extrusion of plastic.

Parts you make yourself are not currently appropriate to put into recycling streams, because the filament typically is not clearly labeled with an appropriate recycling number, nor are the resulting prints. PLA composts in commercial composting facilities (but will not break down at the temperatures of a typical home compost bin). Whereas bottles made from PET plastics are commonly recycled, PET filaments are different formulations, and are not appropriate for the same recycling stream.

Getting Started with Resin Printers

To this point, most of what we have been talking about is specific to the care and feeding of filament-based 3D printers. Resin printers magnify some of these issues. The printers need to be in a very dust-free environment since they can be damaged by small bits of debris in the wrong place at the wrong time. Treat those as you would treat an equivalently priced microscope in terms of clean and stable environment. Do not ever move a resin printer in mid-print.

Complicating matters is the post-processing for resin printers. Different resins and printers require processes that will vary in detail, but go something like this: the print will be created in a tray of resin. When it is done, the platform (on which it has been created upside-down) will be removed from the machine. The print will still be tacky, and the surface may be marred if touched. Figure 5-9 shows a small print on a resin platform. The person doing the post-processing needs to wear chemical-resistant (not latex) gloves, like nitrile ones.

Figure 5-9. *A resin print just out of the printer*

Next, the print needs to be washed and cured. Typically, the wash is done with isopropyl alcohol (various concentrations are advised by manufacturers). The wash alcohol with resin in it needs to be captured for disposal along the way (Figure 5-10).

Figure 5-10. *A resin print being washed with alcohol in a Formlabs wash station*

Finally, the print needs to be UV cured, either in a special box or in the sun. Figure 5-11 shows the print after it has been UV cured and then the supports snipped off. Supports for resin prints tend to be spindly and usually are snipped off with flush cutters or other small cutting tools.

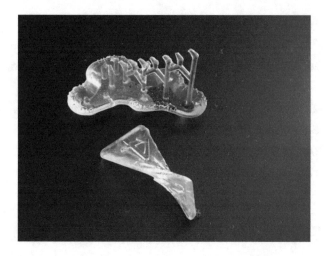

Figure 5-11. *The completed print (and its cut-off supports)*

After the prints are done, the alcohol with dissolved resin needs to be appropriately disposed of, which varies from jurisdiction to jurisdiction. Check with your facilities manager on whether they can handle however much material you will generate, and take a careful look at your manufacturer's instructions.

Also review your manufacturer's requirements for storing resin and disposing of any unused and expired materials.

Staff and User Training

As should be obvious by now, it is challenging to learn how to use a 3D printer on your own. We hope that our books are a good solution if there are no other options, but it is helpful to most people to take a course. We find that two sessions of two hours each work well.

In the first session, we give an overview of the 3D printers that have been purchased, and an introduction to a basic CAD program that the group thinks they want to use. We get them to the point of making a cube or other simple thing and then leave them to play for a week or two. Then we come back and cover the material in Chapter 3, see what has happened in the interim, and get them started with applicable material for what they want to do.

We and others offer online courses on various platforms, which are an option as well—ours can be found at www.nonscriptum.com. Many schools with ambitious maker plans have systems for training and certifying students to run equipment as well.

Summary

This chapter covered the day-to-day issues of supplying and housing a 3D printer and its supplies and associated tools, with a particular emphasis on 3D printers that use filament. We went over basic calibration, facilities issues, and solutions to common problems. We concluded with a review of the basics of resin printers, and touched on staff and user training issues.

CHAPTER 6

3D Models

Your first step in using a 3D printer will be to create a 3D computer model. You do that by scanning an existing object, downloading a model from the web, or creating a model yourself. In each case, there are a lot of options to choose from. There is more to design than picking a software package, though, and there are design decisions you can make that can simplify the printing process.

This chapter first covers the basic file requirements for a 3D printer. Then it reviews options for scanning and downloading 3D models. Finally, the chapter looks at 3D computer-aided design (CAD) and CAD-related programs that you can use to make a 3D model. By the end of the chapter, you should have a computer model that is ready to go on to the next stage of processing. Models can be made from scratch using a 3D CAD program. Some 3D CAD programs are intended for simple beginner projects, but others are more capable (and complex).

Note If starting from zero seems daunting, you might consider downloading a pre-existing model from a database. However, models from these databases often have problems or will not print at all. In Chapter 5, we give the workflow for creating a cube measuring 20 mm on a side. We recommend trying out something like that first before getting into a situation where you do not know if problems are being caused by the model, the slicing settings (Chapter 3), or the printer hardware.

© Joan Horvath, Rich Cameron 2018
J. Horvath and R. Cameron, *Mastering 3D Printing in the Classroom, Library, and Lab*,
https://doi.org/10.1007/978-1-4842-3501-0_6

3D Model File Formats

The term *3D computer model* is used in many different contexts, which can cause confusion when someone wants to print something using a 3D printer. In this book, *3D computer model* means a computer file that contains enough information about the surface of an object to allow the object to be printed. In the open source consumer 3D printer world, the most common file format is the STL file. This acronym is sometimes said to stand for *STereoLithography* and sometimes for *Standard Tessellation Language.*

STL is something of a lowest-common-denominator file format, consisting essentially of a long list of triangles that collectively cover the surface of the object. This is not a terribly efficient format (particularly in its ASCII version, which is a text file), but it has the virtue of being relatively simple to generate and deal with and therefore has become a de facto standard. STL standards exist for both ASCII and binary file versions.

On some Windows computers, you may get an error when saving or moving around an STL file. On Windows, the STL filename extension is presumed to mean Certificate Trust List, and STL files will show up that way in directory listings. STL files will work with 3D printing programs on Windows machines, but sometimes opening the file or saving them will result in an error message complaining about Certificate Trust Lists.

Tip   The open source program MeshLab (discussed under "Mesh Repair Programs" in Chapter 3) is able to translate many different types of files into STL. It can also fix the problems that sometimes occur during translation or as a result of printing incompatibilities in the original model itself.

CT Scans

We introduce the issues with scanning a model in Chapter 3 and discuss commercial scanners. Here we will add a bit to that for scientific users. A scientist may need detailed, high-resolution information about biological structures. Medical professionals and those with access to computerized tomography (CT) scanners have been using CT scans as a starting point for 3D printing. CT scans can capture internal and complex, concave structures. CT scanners are not consumer items, but if you are a scientist or researcher, you might see whether a local hospital or research center offers scans on a fee-for-service basis. Different CT scanners can handle different densities and sizes of objects.

There are also "micro-CT" scanners with smaller beam sizes. University imaging centers and labs buy these smaller scanners for research projects, but often they're not used full-time, and the facilities will do a scan as a fee-for-service arrangement. Facilities with micro-CT scanners are not cheap, and thus neither are these scans. But if you are solving a real problem, micro-CT scanning may be a powerful way to get the information you need to create 3D models of structures of interest.

CT scanners usually output a DICOM file. A web search will reveal various free and proprietary tools to convert DICOM files to STL files, depending on the specific application at hand. One readily available conversion package is InVesalius. Do a web search for their download page, because the software is available in various versions and you may want to hunt around for one that is right for you.

Downloading and Modifying Models

Sometimes a model of something that you would like to print already exists. In that case, you may be able to download it from one of a growing number of model databases. Some databases contain fun

155

items and household objects. Some of the existing models in databases are of complex, specialized objects that might be very useful to you professionally.

Models of Everyday Things

Many databases of 3D-printable objects are available online. The Thingiverse (`www.thingiverse.com`), Youmagine (`www.youmagine.com`), Pinshape (`www.pinshape.com`), and Instructables (`www.instructables.com`) websites all feature a wide range of objects, from sci-fi figurines to parts for enhancing 3D printers. These models have been contributed by users and as such vary widely in the quality of their design both for printing and for their intended purposes.

Sometimes model creators will upload both the STL file for printing and the file in the original format of the software that created the model. That means if you happen to be conversant in the original program, you can start with an object and modify it. For example, in Thingiverse, when you click the Download This Thing! button, you get both a list of the available files and the type of license under which each is being made available. Sometimes the developer just wants you to credit them if you use it. Sometimes commercial use is not allowed. If you obtain something from one of these databases, be sure to look carefully at the requirements, particularly if you're going to modify the object or sell something based on it. See Chapter 3's notes on Creative Commons licenses.

Specialized Databases

Chemists and biologists visualize complex molecules and analyze how these molecules will interact. The Research Collaboratory for Structural Bioinformatics (RCSB) manages the Protein Databank (PDB) at `www.rcsb.org/pdb/`. Anyone can search this databank to find collections of published data about nearly 100,000 protein structures (as of early 2014).

These structures are identified by a PDB ID, which is a four-character alphanumeric code. Once you find the PDB ID, you can use a program that can then take the ID and generate an STL file for printing. The following are two such programs:

- Chimera, from the University of California, San Francisco (`www.cgl.ucsf.edu/chimera/`)

- Visual Molecular Dynamics (VMD), from the University of Illinois at Urbana-Champaign (`www.ks.uiuc.edu/Research/vmd/`)

Both programs have extensive documentation. They are freely available, but have some restrictions on commercial use.

The National Institutes of Health (NIH) in the United States maintains a repository of medicine-related models (`https://3dprint.nih.gov`). The Smithsonian (`https://3d.si.edu`) and other institutions are increasingly putting together "greatest hits" downloadable sets from their collections. Often, though, these files are huge and may have other issues. You will probably want to repair and decimate them — see the section "Repairing a Mesh" in Chapter 3.

Tip   Do not assume that an STL file you download from a site is perfect or that it will work on your printer. It is usually wise to run files through MeshLab (see Tip earlier in this chapter) or a similar program to see if they are watertight and manifold (see Chapter 3) On download sites that allow comments or that have an "I made one!" contribution area, see whether anyone besides the author *has* made one. If not, that might be a bad sign.

Creating a New Model

If you want to print out something that does not exist anywhere, you will need to use software yourself to develop a new model. Fortunately, many software packages are available that make developing particular types of models as simple as possible. This section helps you think about which CAD software package you may want to learn about, if you do not already use one.

Using a CAD Program

Most CAD programs will either save a file as STL directly or offer an option to "export to" STL. Which CAD program is the right one for the job? This section describes commonly used programs ranging in price from open source and/or free to quite expensive. The programs also vary in the steepness of their learning curves. In general, the more powerful the program, the longer it takes to be reasonably proficient in its use.

Some software packages are geared toward creating models meant to be viewed on a computer or theater screen (called *3D rendering*). A "3D" movie normally does not contain the parts of the model that are not on the screen at that moment. Various tricks exploit the way your eyes perceive 3D and fool you into thinking you are seeing a 3D image when really all you are seeing is two offset versions of a 2D image.

If you are at a 3D movie looking at a 3D stereo image of the north side of a tree, that side was generated in a computer. The south side of the tree, the underside of the trunk, and some of the top, east, and west sides are not needed for the movie viewer to see the tree in 3D. However, all of that *is* needed for printing an object. Be sure the software you are looking into can export an STL file or a format that can be converted into STL.

Some programs have the user write computer-code–like instructions, whereas others require a lot of mouse use and more of an artistic bent. This is a quick overview of some of the available options; for the most part,

158

the open source programs offer extensive documentation available for free download. The proprietary software programs typically offer training or have help available.

Options for Getting Started Quickly

If you want to go from "zero to plastic" as soon as possible, you might try Tinkercad (`www.tinkercad.com`) and OpenSCAD (`www.openscad.org`), both of which are free. Tinkercad requires registration; OpenSCAD is open source. Both have example files available that you can play with and use as guidelines for your own first project.

Tinkercad: Drag and Drop

If you want to use something simple that requires no programming knowledge at all, you will like Tinkercad. Tinkercad is a member of Autodesk's suite of 3D printing productivity tools. The program is free as of this writing, although it requires the user to register. Tinkercad is a purely drag-and-drop program that supplies a lot of simple shapes such as rectangular solids, spheres, cylinders, three-dimensional letters of the alphabet, numbers, and so on. Printable objects are created by assembling them out of these standard virtual pieces.

Tinkercad requires a good Internet connection because the program is entirely cloud-based and frequently saves incrementally. If several people are using it on one wifi node, the result can be frozen screens and frustration. However, it's a great way to develop something quickly just to test the end-to-end process of creating a model, slicing it, and printing it. Figure 6-1 shows a simple "star and Saturn" pendant designed by Joan in Tinkercad.

Figure 6-1. *Saturn and star pendant*

Tinkercad has extensive tutorials that are arranged into bite-sized brief walkthroughs of the key features, and there are a lot of examples that others have designed and put out there for you to play with and build upon. The classic project to try first on a 3D printer is a small keychain fob decorated with 3D initials or a few hearts. Most people can do a project of that scale in an hour or so starting from zero with Tinkercad. In Chapter 5, we suggest just printing a cube from Tinkercad as an end-to-end plastic "hello world."

To get started in Tinkercad, follow the process at the Tinkercad home page, `www.tinkercad.com`. Autodesk also has special accounts for teachers to register their students; click the Learn tab for details. First, you will need to create an account (with Autodesk) to use the program. There are good tutorials on the site that appear by default when you go in for the first time.

When you feel comfortable, you can close the tutorial and click "Create new design" to open a new open build plate. You can drag the preexisting shapes onto the build plate, select two or more of them, and use the group icon to merge them into more complex building blocks. You can make any shape a hole (negative space) by selecting the shape you want to use as a hole and then clicking the "hole" graphic. By adding and subtracting shapes, you can build up fairly complex models.

Tinkercad also has features that are new as of this writing – scribble and a coding capability. We describe those in some detail in Chapter 11.

Save your model by clicking the Export button and selecting the option to download for 3D printing. Laser cutting is an option too, for models that can be made as a flat cutout.

You should now have an STL file in your downloads folder that you can import into your slicer of choice (see Chapter 3) and ultimately print. Tinkercad makes up weird, pseudo-Swedish names for models. You can make them something more memorable by clicking the name it made up and typing in what you would like to call it. Alternatively, you can take one of the public Tinkercad models and alter it a bit, if the model creator allows that, and then save it to STL. Remember to start small and simple—see the "3D Printing Design Rules" section at the end of this chapter about what makes a model "simple."

Tinkercad also has the ability to model basic circuits and create enclosures for some electronics components in your 3D print. See www.tinkercad.com/circuits for details.

Note   There are a variety of other low-cost, school-oriented CAD programs, and more pop up all the time. Morphi (www.morphiapp.com) has a small cost per seat, but does not require a live wifi connection (which Tinkercad does). People sometimes try to use Inkscape (https://inkscape.org) for 3D printing, but it is not designed for it, and you will need to export your drawing to another program to extrude it into the third dimension. The result after all that will be better suited for a laser cutter.

OpenSCAD: A CAD Programming Environment

OpenSCAD follows the opposite philosophy from Tinkercad in that it is not drag and drop at all, except for adjusting how you view the model you have developed. OpenSCAD uses a programming language very similar to C to define geometrical shapes, translations, rotations, and so on.

The program has built-in functions for most common shapes, although the names can be a little misleading. For example, all the rectangular solids are called "cubes." Figure 6-2 shows a simple file with three "cubes" assembled into a simple bridge by moving (*translating*) the top and one side of the bridge away from the zero point. Note that the cubes were designed to be slightly overlapping—because shapes with purely coincident faces may not have created a manifold STL.

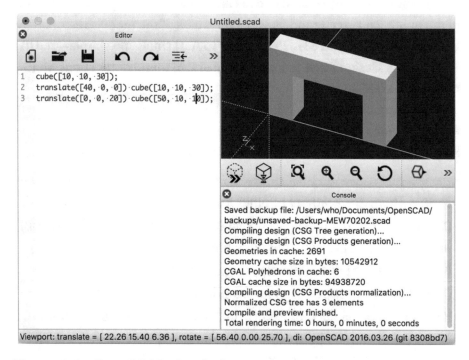

Figure 6-2. *OpenSCAD simple demonstration*

To try out a simple model in OpenSCAD, first either click File ➤ New to start a new model or pick an example from the Example submenu. You can also type in the little example shown in Figure 6-2—the three lines shown are all you need for the model shown. As with any program, saving frequently is a good idea, which you do from the File menu. This will save the program in OpenSCAD format, not STL.

If you want to see what your model will look like, select Design ➤ Preview. This creates a quick visualization of your model without taking the time to calculate all the geometry.

Click and drag with your mouse in the preview pane to roll your model around and see it from different angles. This is also useful to give you a better idea of what the shape actually looks like in 3D.

If you like the looks of what you see in the 3D preview, you'll want to render the model and create an STL. Go back to Design ➤ Render. This may take longer than the preview step (especially if your model is very complex or uses certain computationally-intensive elements), which is why the preview is available.

When rendering has finished, the preview pane will update. If you had used colors or certain other features, you may notice that they disappear, because they are not supported by STL and thus are only usable for previewing. Roll your model around in the 3D view again and make sure it still looks like you expect. If it does, go to File ➤ Export and then choose STL as the file format.

You can then take the STL file and run it through a slicing program (see Chapter 3) and you will be ready to print. OpenSCAD is particularly suited to modeling objects that can be built up out of geometric shapes. Complex objects are possible by starting with these basic shapes and rotating them. You can make impressive geometries with a little programming experience and the OpenSCAD manual. We have two books of 3D printed science and math models, all of which were created in OpenSCAD (*3D Printed Science Models* (Apress, 2016) and *3D Printed Science Models Volume 2* (Apress, 2017). Figure 6-3 shows a botanical model from the "Plants and their Ecosystems" chapter of the 2016 book.

Tip   It is helpful if you create an STL and export it in the orientation you expect to print it in. Consider minimizing support. One special case is thin objects with a lot of surface detail, like the models in Figure 6-3. In that case, you may want to print the objects standing on end, as these were printed. As long as the overhangs are manageable, this should work well.

Figure 6-3. *Botanical model (agave plant) from 3D Printed Science Models (Apress, 2016)*

Programs for Specific Applications

Tinkercad and OpenSCAD are great for beginners. If you are using your printer mostly as a hobbyist, in a classroom, or to make fun objects around the house, you can probably be happy for a long time with these programs. However, if you need to create professional-level sculptural models, or if you need dimensioned drawings, then these programs probably are not enough. Many, many design programs can either produce an STL file or a file that can be translated into STL. Most of these programs deserve (and in some cases have) their own book-length tutorials.

Generally speaking, you need to consider a few key attributes when selecting a design program. First, think about your own strengths: are you good at programming, or are you better at drawing with a mouse? Do you have decent hand-eye coordination and drawing skills? How much time do you have to devote to becoming proficient, and how much design are you really going to do? A program with a short learning curve but limited capability may be okay if you are only going to make a few complicated objects, but learning a more-capable program may be worth it if those features will vastly enhance your productivity.

Some software only runs on either Mac or Windows, not both. If you only have access to one or the other operating system, that may force a choice.

Next, consider budget. Free and open source software varies in quality; documentation can be uneven or incomplete for open source software. However, it *is* free. For pricey software, research whether demonstration versions of the software are available, and if so, try before you buy. If you are a student, check with your school to see whether any discounts are available to you.

With all that said, programs to create models for 3D printing need to serve various constituencies. Engineers, architects, industrial designers, mathematicians, and similar professionals need drawings with each part's dimensions shown and great precision. Often, they will need to integrate 3D printed parts with traditionally manufactured ones and thus will need both the ability to create a file for printing and a traditionally dimensioned, human-readable drawing. Artists may want good drawing tools that allow them to sketch freely but not require as much precision. Different tools have evolved for these respective communities, as we will see next.

Engineering and Architecture Programs

Engineers, industrial designers, and architects use 3D modeling programs oriented toward applications that require precision. A relatively new arrival on the engineering CAD scene is Onshape (`www.onshape.com`). Onshape is cloud based and free for many educational uses. It has a growing suite of plug-ins for modeling and analysis. It runs in a browser, so it runs on Chromebooks, Macs, and Windows and Linux machines, and it also has apps for iOS and Android devices.

Fusion360 (`www.autodesk.com/products/fusion-360`) is Autodesk's entry in this category. Autodesk used to have a line of CAD programs called "123D...". The simpler end of these applications has been rolled into Tinkercad, and the more sophisticated, into Fusion360. Fusion360 has some CAM (computer-aided manufacturing) capability included. It also has (confusingly) a "slicer" function, but it slices models into pieces suitable for laser cutting as interlocking pieces. As of this writing, its CAM abilities were limited to CNC machines, and not 3D printers. The program is free for many educational and personal applications at the moment; see the website for terms and conditions, or to purchase it.

A common (but expensive) engineering tool is Solidworks, from Dassault Systèmes (`www.solidworks.com`). Solidworks is designed to create real engineering projects and as such is a good end-to-end program to go from concept to final dimensioned parts. It does take a while to become proficient in Solidworks, though, and cost can be a barrier once one is beyond the reach of educational discounts. Solidworks is only available for Windows (although there is a free viewer called eDrawings that works on Macs).

Sketchup (`www.sketchup.com`) is a program focused on making it easy to lay out an architectural project, including a large library of many common home fixtures from various manufacturers. Sketchup can be used more broadly, but it focuses mostly on assembling geometrical and precise models, and the resulting models may require format conversion and have problems with 3D printing.

Mathematica (www.wolfram.com/mathematica/) is a programming system that allows users to model complicated mathematical functions. Mathematica creates STL files based on user-generated mathematical models. That means it's possible to develop sophisticated mathematical models and then visualize them in physical form. This possibility has many implications, particularly for people who teach courses that use Mathematica. A natural spectrum of mathematics visualization options starts with OpenSCAD and moves up to Mathematica.

Visual-Effects and Sculptural Programs

Visual-effects developers, animators, and similar artists develop 3D models in computer programs that are good for complex, curved, organic objects such as characters in animated films. Most of these either can export an STL file directly or employ translation utilities and procedures to take their output and turn it into STL. The commercial program Rhino, for example, exports directly into STL.

Zbrush (www.zbrush.com) is another commercial program for artists. It's a complex but very capable program that allows the user to sculpt in virtual clay. Users often abandon the mouse and draw instead on a graphic tablet with a stylus to create very sophisticated, realistic designs of animated characters and the like.

Blender is an open source visual-effects development program, available from www.blender.org. It is extremely powerful—you can make an entire animated film with it—but has a correspondingly steep learning curve. If you are very fast with a mouse, this may be the program for you, but the program is notorious for "thinking" differently from all other programs. It is, however, free.

Tip   If you are interested in creating 3D models with Blender, you might try to locate a class or, even better, a local Blender community or Meetup group. Lynda.com/LinkedIn Learning has online Blender courses.

Maya (www.autodesk.com/products/maya), an animation program, exports OBJ files that some slicing programs, including Cura 3, can read. However, Maya is a mesh-based modeler. That means when you draw something, you are creating a "mesh" that defines surfaces rather than working with geometric solids and letting the software generate their surfaces.

For example, if you model a ball and cut it in half, you are creating a cup-shaped hemispherical surface, facing outward, but it doesn't have an inward-facing surface, and does not enclose any volume. The software later in the 3D-printing workflow will do unpredictable things with this. You need to use the solidify functions of the modeling software to give your mesh some thickness, or add faces to the open sides to create a half-sphere. Once you are sure your mesh has no holes connecting the inside to the outside, and that the surface does not intersect with itself, you can safely export it as an OBJ file.

Because programs like Maya or Blender are intended only for creating models that will look right when rendered as 2D images, the user has to do some extra work to ensure that the models it produces will be manifold. You will have to make sure that your meshes are all closed and have no unnecessary internal geometry or self-intersections, or your slicing program and printer might both do unpredictable things.

If you want to turn a 2D surface into a printable mesh, you will need to *extrude* or "solidify" it so that it has a thickness of at least a millimeter or two. Be sure you are working in millimeters first or you might make inch- or centimeter-thick walls!

Tip   As of this writing, Maya comes with a plug-in that generates OBJ files, but the plug-in by default is not enabled. Use Maya's Plugin Manager to enable the OBJexport plug-in so you can then export Maya's native format to OBJ files.

Creating Multiple-Extruder Files

A printer with dual extruders allows you to print in two colors or, in some cases, two materials. Exactly how this works depends a lot on the dual extruder machine in question, but this general guide will give you some ideas on how to get started with your machine. You can use a dual extruder machine in a couple of different ways. First, you can use a different color of the same material in each extruder. You can also load one extruder with a dissolvable support material so that you can just wash off support. You may also be able to combine different materials with different properties, or your printer may have the ability to use the second extruder in parallel to make two identical objects. There are now several different types of multi-extruder setups, each with its own capabilities and caveats.

Using One Extruder for Support Material

If you are printing something with significant amounts of support material, you may want to simplify the removal of that support. Dissolvable support is made for this purpose. In this case, no extra steps are necessary prior to sending an STL file to your slicing program (Chapter 3). You will need to tell the slicer which extruder is using the support material.

Water-soluble support filament is usually relatively expensive, and may come in smaller quantities (both for cost reasons and because it can be ruined by leaving it out to absorb moisture from the air). For this reason, it can be advantageous to minimize how much of it you use. Most slicers now have the ability to configure the extruder used for the support interface separately from the rest of the support structures, which allows you to print the bulk of the supports with the cheaper print material and only use the soluble material for the interface between the supports and the part. Depending on the geometry and orientation of your part and of its support structures, this may allow the supports to just fall off, or some breaking of the supports might still be required to remove them, but it makes support removal easier and less likely to mar the surface of your part than using break-away supports.

If your printer has multiple extruders that share a single nozzle, you may find there is no way to use them for materials with different properties, or if you can, that it requires significant purging of the extruder to switch back and forth. Using a support material that is formulated to have similar printing temperatures to your print material will help.

Two-Color or Two-Material Prints

As mentioned, dual-extruder printers allow you to print objects in two colors or materials. It is still a little complicated, though. First, you need to create the STL files for each of the extruders separately, so that you can assign each one to an extruder. In the example here, we will be printing a red heart pendant with a light blue star and exclamation point. This entire object was created in Tinkercad, with the exclamation point, star, and heart all in the same file.

To create a two-color object, we needed to create two separate STL files. To create the first one, we turned the heart/pendant hook into a "hole" in Tinkercad and subtracted it from the merged item to ensure that the two shapes would not overlap. We then saved that much into what we will call STL number 1.

Then, to make the second STL, we undid the merging, turned the heart/pendant back into a regular object, and deleted the star and exclamation point so that we could export just that part as STL number 2. Remember to undo the deletion (or better yet, work with a copy of your original file) so that you don't lose the ability to edit your file and try again.

These two STLs are shown in Cura 3 (Figures 6-4 and 6-5) as they look when they are dragged in separately. Note that some of the model in Figure 6-4 is just hanging in air, because the models need to have the same coordinate system as each other to begin with.

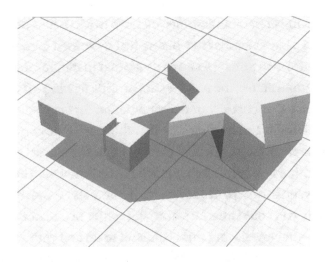

Figure 6-4. *The first of two models to be merged in a dual extruder print*

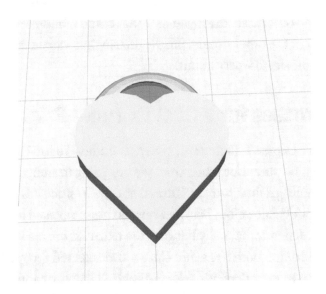

Figure 6-5. *The second model*

While making these two files, we were careful not to move anything around during this process so that the STL files would line up properly when we re-merged them.

The following directions assume you have two STL files that were created with a process similar to what we just described for our heart pendant—that is, two STLs created in a way that maintains the same coordinate system across the two files and avoids overlaps. If your printer has multiple nozzles, check your documentation for determining the offset between them and making sure that they are at the correct relative heights. For some printers, you will need to enter the correct offset values in the slicer; others carry this information in the firmware. The offset is the distance between the two extruder heads in the x and y directions.

In a pinch, you could measure from the center of one nozzle to the center of the other nozzle, but this is difficult to do and your manufacturer should have given you either a number or a means of determining the number from a print. Unless your printer has some method of moving the inactive nozzle out of the way, height adjustments will need to be made mechanically—otherwise, the lower extruder could collide with the plastic that came out of the other nozzle. Single-nozzle dual extruder systems do not have any offsets to worry about.

Cura's Process for a Dual Extruder Print

As we note in Chapter 3, slicing software gets updated a lot. However, the general processes stay about the same. We are going to walk through the process of creating a dual print in Ultimaker Cura 3, since it is so tightly tied to the model generation. For the example here, we used a MAKEiT Pro 3D printer, which automatically handles the extruder offsets in firmware.

First, we brought both STLs into Cura 3 and selected the MAKEiT Pro M, which has two extruders. We selected each STL in turn and chose an extruder for it (Figure 6-7). Then we right-clicked one of the models and selected Select All Models and then Merge Models. The result is Figure 6-8.

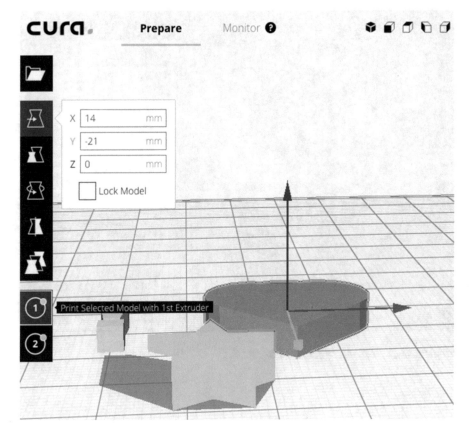

Figure 6-6. *Assigning an extruder to an STL*

Finally, under the Dual Extrusion settings (visible in Figures 6-7 and 6-8), we added a prime tower and an ooze shield. This figure highlights a single layer simulation in Cura, with the tower and shield (you have to select "show helpers" to see these) and the travel among them shown in light purple.

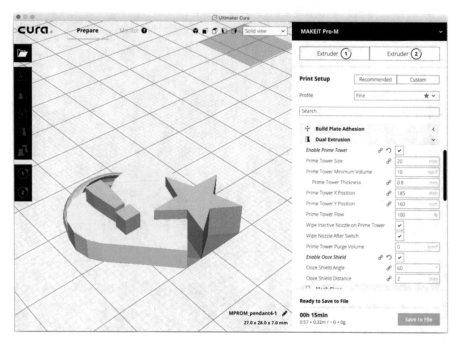

Figure 6-7. *The merged STLs*

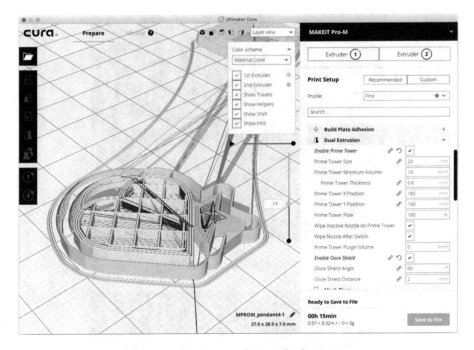

Figure 6-8. *A simulation partway through the print*

These features, visible in the photos in Figures 6-9 and 6-10 taken during printing, keep the extruder not being used from dripping plastic onto the print when it is supposed to be idle.

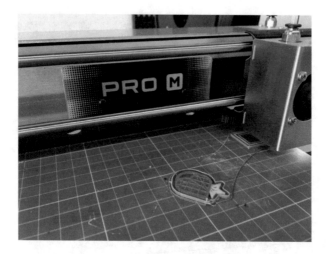

Figure 6-9. *The dual extruder print in process*

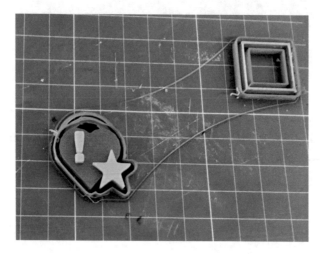

Figure 6-10. *The completed print on the printer*

The prime tower can get a little uneven and get knocked off near the end; if that happens near the end of a long print, you can let the print finish just drooling over where the prime tower was as long as the prime tower wound up somewhere out of the way. Note that the wipe shield curves around the print and does not go straight up. Figure 6-11 shows the print after it has been removed from the platform and separated from the wipe shield.

Figure 6-11. *The final print*

3D Printing Design Rules

Chapter 3 discusses the software used to create commands for a printer given an STL model. Sometimes minor design changes can make a big difference in how well your print will come out. In 3D printing, the devil is in the details. This section offers a few things to keep in mind when you are designing a 3D print. Then we go into a few philosophical issues about what you can do with a 3D printer that uniquely exploits the value of the technology.

Here are a few design rules to keep in mind when developing models for 3D printing with filament:

- Know your printer's minimum feature size; for most printers, this will be around 1 mm. Anything smaller will be marginal to print, particularly in the plane of the platform.

- Prints can be hollow (as long as the internal overhangs can be bridged), or they can have any infill percentage up to and including solid (100%).

- To make a print sturdier, first up the number of perimeters before increasing the percentage infill.

- Fine detail should be printed on the side of a print for maximum resolution.

- Minimize support by cutting your model into pieces, reorienting it, and so on, while maximizing contact with the build platform. Overhangs of up to about 45 degrees can be handled without support.

- If the print is functional and will be stressed, orient it so that loads are in the plane of the platform, not stressing the layer-to-layer bond. (More on this in Chapter 9.)

- If you are going to be sanding or otherwise finishing a print in a way that will remove material, or if you will be adding a filler to the surface to smooth it out, allow for that in the print.

- 10 mm holes are too small for 10 mm parts to fit inside. Leave at least 0.1 mm tolerance as a general rule. You may need more or less depending on your printer, the layer height you are using, the facet size of your model, and how much resistance you want between the two parts, to name a few factors.

- Bear in mind the heat, UV light, and chemical sensitivity of your print if it will be used in environments where those things matter. PLA will warp in a hot window in summer, and will deform over time even at room temperature if there is a constant load on it.

- Print tall, skinny parts with a cooling tower (Chapter 8).

- If a model has a thin part (such as a fin), try to add perimeters until the thin part is solid and work out the thickness so that an even number of perimeters fits, if you have flexibility on sizes. Otherwise infill might be spotty and uneven and distort the surface.

For resin printers, somewhat different rules apply:

- For resin printing, support can be a virtue. Design your model so that the contact area with the platform is minimal, because those layers may be compressed or distorted. To minimize support scarring and peel force, it is often best to print a flat object at 45 degrees in resin.

- Resin prints should not have completely enclosed hollow spaces or bowl-shaped areas that could trap resin or air during the print. If they do, the geometry has to have a hole to allow the resin to flow.

- Because the prints are more isotropic and can handle smaller features, resolution and strength issues are less of a driver for most resin prints.

- Different thermal, chemical, and UV exposure issues affect resins. Because there is now a large range of types of resin, you will need to understand the environmental requirements of your particular resin.

Caution   Most CAD programs and 3D printers use millimeters as a default. Be careful that you do not accidentally save a file in inches, since your print might be interpreted as a teeny version of itself when the slicer opens it and interprets inches as millimeters.

Complexity Is Free: Hardware as a Service

One of the mantras of the 3D-printer community is that *complexity is free*. Because 3D-printed parts are built up one layer at a time, it really doesn't matter whether that layer is one unbroken sheet or an intricate design. There are models that would be essentially impossible to machine, but people who know what they are doing can print them on a low-cost consumer printer.

Consumer-level printers have one more strong advantage: the opportunity to iteratively design something, see how it came out, and then change the design if necessary. When that became possible in the 1980s for computing (versus overnight batch jobs), there was a real change to the nature of creating software. We all hope the same thing is about to happen for making physical things!

This phenomenon is starting to be called *hardware as a service* (an analogy to *software as a service*), and the business models are still unclear. Resolution and materials are likely to continue improving, and all the pictures in this book will probably look primitive to anyone reading this a few years down the road. Chapter 14 speculates on how 3D-printing businesses may evolve toward short-run manufacturing or mass customization.

Speed vs. Customization

Complexity is not entirely free because the amount of material used (and the time it takes to print) is more proportional to surface area than to volume of the part. Complexity may matter less in 3D printing than in conventional fabrication, but complex prints may take a long time. Consumer 3D printers take a while to print anything out—it's rare for a print of any size to take less than a few hours, and prints that take a day are routine. If you're making one of something or a prototype for a mold, such a length of time may be competitive. The other option is a machinist or other professional making a prototype in a way that involves a lot of labor. But if the part is simple or you want a lot of them, a 3D-printed part is probably not the way to go. If you are happily creating injection-molded parts for something now, then 3D-printing that part is *definitely* not the way to go.

To narrow it down a bit more, consumer 3D printers may not be the best fit for your project if everything you do will require a lot of hand finishing after the fact. You might consider using a service bureau to do one of the more industrial processes. To put it another way, only the right kind of complexity is free.

3D printing has a role for items that are by their nature one-of-a-kind (or a-few-of-a-kind) and that work well with the technology. Time will tell what the best applications are. Our sense is that one key role for 3D printing is that it makes the front of the product-development process faster. People who would have made a computer model and then created a foam-core physical mockup as two separate chores are obviously better off with a 3D printer.

Other promising markets exist in industries that make custom parts for one-of-a-kind applications (or, even better, industries that *should* operate that way but cannot do so economically at the moment). The biggest market now, though, is a somewhat intangible one: allowing people to make stuff again just because they want to and can.

Summary

In this chapter, you learned about the beginning of the 3D-printing process. The first step is creating or finding a 3D digital model of your object, which requires you to visit a website with objects available for download, 3D-scan something that already exists, or learn one of the many available 3D modeling software packages. The chapter went over the various types of software packages available for the engineer versus the artist to generate a standard (STL) 3D-printing file and some rules of thumb about best design practices for 3D printing.

PART III

3D Printing Curriculum Development

Part 3 (Chapters 7–12) discuss the use of 3D printing in different subject disciplines, with a particular focus on the K–12 classroom. We start off with a brief introduction to common issues in classroom 3D printing, and then look at art and theater concerns, considering print post-processing topics like gluing, sanding, and painting, as well as a bit about casting jewelry. Then we consider engineering concerns, such as making a print strong enough for a functional job. Next we take up using printers in language arts and social studies, and in the elementary school environment. Finally, we talk about how 3D prints might help special-needs students, particularly the visually impaired.

CHAPTER 7

Classroom Issues

To this point, we have been focusing on the mechanics of choosing and using a 3D printer. However, the mechanics of using a printer to produce a good print is just a start. Deciding how to use the technology effectively is challenging, too. In this chapter, we discuss some issues common to most educational settings. In the remaining chapters of the book, we discuss particular opportunities and challenges for different disciplines and age groups.

Workflow

Most teachers have not dealt with digital fabrication tools (3D printers, CNC machines, laser cutters, and so on) before encountering them in a makerspace. Marketing videos usually show a time lapse of an object magically appearing on a build platform. The reality, though, is different. A modest print can take hours or even days, depending on the printer, the material, and the geometry of the print.

For filament-based printers, there are limits to how much faster the technology will get, based on physics. One layer has to cool enough for the next one to be laid down, and fans can only do so much. So these will always be slow. There are (currently exotic) techniques to do resin prints faster, but they are extremely expensive.

© Joan Horvath, Rich Cameron 2018
J. Horvath and R. Cameron, *Mastering 3D Printing in the Classroom, Library, and Lab*,
https://doi.org/10.1007/978-1-4842-3501-0_7

Time to Print

Most methods of one-at-a-time 3D fabrication are pretty slow, even for a professional practitioner. We talked about laser cutters and CNC machines versus 3D printers in Chapter 1 and will not repeat those tradeoffs here. Consider the time it might take for a person to carve the same shape with hand tools, and perhaps it might not seem slow at all!

All this does not help, though, when you have a 50-minute class period with 30 students and you want to involve all of them in making a 3D print. Here are a few options:

- Have each student make something small, and print them in batches. Because of the cooling-time issue, often several small objects take the same time to print as one small object.

- Only 3D print what really needs to be 3D printed. If a student is making a sculpture that will stand on a big cube of a base, use something else for the base and only print the sculpture.

- Have 3D printing as part of a group project, and have one 3D printed part per group. Ideally, have this project spread over several weeks or stagger group project stages somehow to spread out demand.

- Teach good design practices that minimize support.

- Have a review process that sends prints that will fail or use inordinate resources back to the student, with feedback and an opportunity for the student to fix the design problem. This also spreads out the load on the printers if a lot of prints bounce on first submittal, but overall class timelines will need to allow for this.

There are philosophical questions to consider, too. For example, will you allow a student to print something they have downloaded from a database and not changed in any way? Can they include such a file in their projects, or do you want to require that anything they print on a school printer has at least some original work? Or, perhaps, will you only allow them to print things they have designed from scratch? Are there things you will forbid your students to print? If you are new to this, you might check with a peer school that is ahead of you to see what has worked for them.

Print Queue Management

If you have a lot of students creating files to print, managing the optimal use of the printers you have can be challenging. You will need to create a priority system. Even if it's just "first come, first served," write it down and post it. Do classroom projects have priority over after-school activities, like the robotics team? Here are some options for managing priorities based on the type of print job:

- Short jobs cut the queue ahead of long ones.

- Small jobs wait until they can be plated together and printed at once.

- Risky experiments might wait until no class projects are due for a few days.

You will also need a way to track which prints are waiting to be printed, have been printed, have been attempted but have had the print fail, or have been rejected without printing for technical reasons. It is best to keep the sliced file until you are sure the print worked; otherwise you might need to waste time slicing it again if something went wrong (like a power outage) that does not require changing anything before printing again.

Finally, you will need to decide what to do about prints that take more than one school day. Will you allow overnight (or over-weekend) printing? If, say, the robotics team meets after school and only has a few hours, can they start a print and have it finish unattended? At any rate, you should get a fair amount of experience before leaving a printer unattended for any length of time so you know what will fail. You might come back to find a mess you have to clean up.

Many people put a webcam on their printer so they know if something has gone very wrong and can sprint over and deal with it. If you have a remote interface like Octoprint (Chapter 3), you can even stop the print remotely if you see that something has gone wrong. You will still have to remove the print and clean up whatever mess it made before you can try again, though.

Curriculum Issues

We are often asked where to find "maker curriculum" materials. We always find the request a little odd, because it seems to us that the right thing to do is to use tools like 3D printing to enhance learning in the typical subjects, rather than treat it like something to be learned per se.

Constructivist Seymour Papert famously suggested that student projects needed to have a low floor and a high ceiling, by which he meant that students should be able to at least get a toehold in a concept if they are struggling, but that there should be a lot of flexibility for stronger students to explore to the limits of their ability.

Right now, 3D printing's "low floor" is seen as finding and downloading an existing model. This is unfortunately a common model of "using 3D printing in the curriculum." We feel that designing a model—or perhaps altering ones that get you started—is where a lot of the learning takes place. For examples, see Chapter 9's discussion about our science and math models and the philosophy behind them.

Except in some specialized cases (like teaching the visually impaired, as we describe in Chapter 12) just downloading a model and printing it probably does not add much value and is more or less a new version of ordering a model from a supply house. Database models can be misleading or represent a concept incorrectly, too.

So the question becomes: can students use Tinkercad, say, to have just a bit higher floor to visualize something they have just learned about, or to express themselves creatively? More importantly, how does doing this serve having them learn what they are trying to learn?

Currently, we are working on a project to reimagine calculus from zero and to create a hands-on version we call "Hacker Calculus." It has become clear that to do it right one has to throw out the usual order of teaching. Time will tell how well this works!

What "Design Thinking" Means

Joan is trained as an aeronautical engineer and worked for 16 years as a rocket scientist. In that role she participated in many design meetings. Rich designed one of the earliest ancestors of today's consumer 3D printers, as well as a modern consumer device. If you are teaching "design thinking" in a middle-school context, you may be confronted with many charts of the process that are wonders of color and complexity. Some we have seen would have given people planning missions to Venus pause, or made them roll their eyes.

Design is something we all do every day, and it does not have to be, well, rocket science. A generic design process goes something like this:

- Figure out what you want to do, or what problem you are trying to solve (without stating, yet, how you want to do it). Engineers call this "specifying requirements and not implementation," which means: "Tell me what you need my design to do, and stop telling me how to do it."

- Think about what makes a design "the best" for this purpose and what "success" is and how to measure it. (Who decides what is "best"?)

- Next, come up with some ways to do what needs to be done. Pick the one that seems "best" (given #2) and try it.

- Did it work, by your definition of success? You are good! If not, roll back as far as you have to and try again.

Making the process itself something to learn, with terminology and vocabulary and many steps and arrows, seems to us to defeat the purpose of encouraging students to explore and prototype, and it can also intimidate teachers. Keep it simple and commonsense. Clear metrics of success can help with figuring out how to grade a project, too.

One reason why 3D printing and its sister digital fabrication technologies are challenging is that they require fluency in both digital design and the realities of what will happen when that design is created (or not) with an imperfect machine using real-world materials. The latter takes some amount of experience and willingness to live with failures along the way. Being able to live comfortably in both these worlds—to be able to design something that will actually work—will always be an in-demand skill and a key preparation for many STEM careers. But it requires an orderly approach and some discipline to get things to work.

It is still early days for us all to figure out the implications of this in the K-12 environment. For more on the big picture about 3D printing and the future workforce, see Chapter 14.

Summary

In this chapter, we discussed issues that arise in working with 3D printing in a school setting, including developing printing policies and workflows. Printer time needs to be managed, and makerspace managers must decide whether or not students need to develop their own designs, versus just printing something that already exists. We also considered how to make the concept of design thinking a bit less intimidating, and closed with some thoughts about the big picture of what students will need to learn now to be competitive in the world in which they will eventually work.

CHAPTER 8

Art and Theater

3D printing is a mixed blessing for artists. Like all media, it has situations where it is particularly powerful, and others where it is limited. The big minus for many artists is the need for a computer model to start with. Some like the texture of layer lines, while others consider them a nonstarter. In this chapter, we discuss some of the issues that arise when printing art objects and theatrical props in particular, from some challenging object shapes to ways to post-process a print for particular effects.

We know that art and theater teachers are often early adopters of 3D printing in their schools, and also are the ones to push the envelope the most on surface quality and unusual geometries. If you teach (or practice) in one of these disciplines, this chapter gives you some idea of what is possible. We hope you will go on to innovate even cooler techniques.

We start off with a discussion of materials and geometries that result in prints that are a little challenging to deal with, and end with a discussion of designing for casting. In-between we cover some of the techniques and products available for finishing a print.

As with the rest of this book, our primary focus in this chapter is on techniques that apply to filament-based printing. In some cases, resin prints start out where filament prints are after the post-processing, due to their superior surface smoothness in the first place. Most materials (except for nylon) can be hand-sanded and painted.

© Joan Horvath, Rich Cameron 2018
J. Horvath and R. Cameron, *Mastering 3D Printing in the Classroom, Library, and Lab*,
https://doi.org/10.1007/978-1-4842-3501-0_8

For resin prints, the composition of "resin" is varied and proprietary to different printers, so for the most part you will need to depend on suggestions from your manufacturer. In this chapter, we point to resources from Formlabs (`www.formlabs.com`), which has extensive material online. However, what works for Formlabs proprietary resins may or may not carry over to your printer, so bear that in mind as you read on.

Note   Our book with Lyn Hoge, *Practical Fashion Tech* (Apress, 2016), discusses a variety of other techniques to create technical costumes that go beyond the 3D printing–centric suggestions here.

Specialty Materials

One way to get particular effects in your prints is to use a novel material. However, not every printer can use every filament or resin. In the case of filament printers, one way to get interesting surface effects is to use a *filled filament*. These are typically PLA-based filaments with metal or wood powder mixed in. The filaments can be challenging to use, with a tendency to clog the nozzle, and the metal or fiber ones can abrade a nozzle. But the effects can give the appearance of wood or metal.

Figure 8-1 shows four pieces that were printed and then sanded with many progressively finer grits of sandpaper. The top left and lower right pieces are plain PLA. The upper right is steel-filled PLA, and the lower left is wood-filled. Filled PLA can be printed on blue tape at PLA temperatures.

Figure 8-1. *Sanded PLA pieces*

Flexible filaments made of various elastomers also are readily available. They can be challenging to print, though, because they can tend to jam (particularly in machines that use 1.75 mm filament and Bowden tubes). However, if you can get past that, you can make some pretty interesting flexible objects.

In the case of resin printers, it is difficult to generalize because a lot of the differentiation from manufacturer to manufacturer is in development of specialty resins. Resins exist that are flexible, particularly durable, suitable for high-temperature applications like making injection molds, and more. Your choice of a resin printer is likely to be driven in part by what type of material you want to use. (See detailed discussions of this in Chapters 2 and 4.)

Challenging Geometries

Not every print is equally hard to create. There are a few special cases that require particular setups, and because they arise often in art projects and theatrical prop-making, we cover them in this chapter. These prints involve extremes in one physical property or another—hollow, or completely solid, or thin, or otherwise a shape that pushes the envelope of filament printing.

Vase Prints

Slicing programs allow us to specify how many solid layers are on the top or bottom of a print, as opposed to the interior of the print that is partially filled with an infill pattern (Chapter 3). But suppose you want a print that is solid on the bottom and otherwise open, like a vase? As it happens, most slicing programs have a "spiral vase mode" that prints a specified number of bottom layers, and then spirals up an outer contour that is just one perimeter thick. In Ultimaker Cura 3 this is a check box: Special Modes ➤ Spiralize Outer Contour. The vases in Figure 8-2 were created this way.

There is also a fun option for vases: Special Modes ➤ Fuzzy Skin. The right-hand vase in Figure 8-2 used the two options together to produce a textured vase.

Figure 8-2. *Two spiralized vases, the one on the right with "fuzzy skin"*

There is also "old-school vase mode," which explicitly specifies zero infill and no top layers, which is how vases were printed before slicers had special modes for that purpose. The difference is that in old-school vase mode, you do not have the continuous spiral that theoretically removes all seams (though in some cases, spiral mode actually makes the seams more visible). The old-school version also allows you to have layers with multiple islands or with holes (which in spiral mode would either result in unpredictable behavior or throw an error), and you can also use multiple perimeters to create a thicker-walled vase (which also makes it easier to make it water-tight).

Other Uses of Vase Mode

Vase mode can come in handy if you are printing something very thin with surface detail on both sides. If you print such a thing vertically you might find yourself with gaps and other issues. For example, the gravitational wave print from our book *3D Printed Science Projects Volume 2* (Apress, 2015) had areas where it was not quite the right thickness for either never or always having some infill, and some gaps resulted.

We tried printing it with the "spiralize outer contour" feature and in essence created a "vase" with a 1 mm-wide opening at the top. Figure 8-3 shows this print, in translucent PLA.

Figure 8-3. *Gravitational waves, printed as vases*

The print bed holds two different waves, each of which is a vase open at the top. (This particular print was pushing the envelope of vase printing. Printing two items at once like this may or may not work.)

Printing Hollow

It is a short step from printing a vase to considering printing something hollow. Normally you would not want to do that, but if for some reason you do, just set infill to 0%. You may want to increase the number of perimeters for stability of the model. Figure 8-4 shows a hollow model with modest enough overhangs that it could be printed just as a shell.

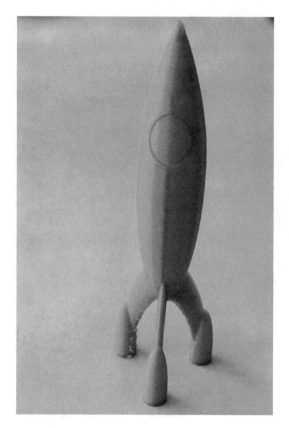

Figure 8-4. *A hollow print*

Printing Transparent (Solid) Pieces

There are now some filaments available that offer high degrees of transparency, but a typical print has too many air bubbles for you to see through it. If you print on a smooth surface, you may be able to see into the bottom of the print very clearly, but the top surface, where the print had to bridge over the infill, will be irregular enough that it will not be very clear. If you try to look through the side of the print, you will be able to see where the infill lines meet the wall, but the rounded edges of the layers will distort your view.

Even if you sand the sides smooth or use special transparent coatings to fill in the gaps and smooth the surface, the layer lines on the interior will still create this distortion. Only a print created completely solid can be as transparent as the ones shown in Figure 8-5.

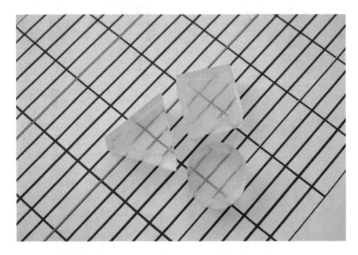

Figure 8-5. *Transparent prints*

Therefore, the only way to print transparent objects is usually to print them solid. A 3D print generally consists of solid surfaces that are around 1 mm thick, with the interior filled with sparser infill structures. Your slicing software probably has a setting for how many solid top and bottom layers you want. To make a print solid, just increase this number until all layers are solid layers.

Printing solid can be finicky, though, because it makes the printer much more sensitive to small errors in the amount of plastic being extruded. If you are extruding slightly too much, melted plastic can build up around the nozzle. In a regular print, this buildup would even out once you got to the sparse infill, but that does not happen when you are printing solid.

It is also challenging to print a clear piece on blue tape or other textured surfaces, because the pattern from the surface will keep the print from being smooth. For best results, you may need a printer that has a heated platform and a surface that is not noticeably rough.

You can lower the fudge factor called the *extrusion multiplier* in some slicers (*flow* in Cura 3) to a slightly lower number, like 95 to 98% from its default of 100%. On the other hand, if your extrusion multiplier is a bit too low, you will end up with a print that has most of the strength of a solid print but is full of tiny bubbles and air channels where there was not quite enough plastic to fill the space, and these will prevent the print from being transparent. It is also important to print slowly, to allow all the air to escape. If you want to do a lot of transparent prints, you may be better off using a resin printer with transparent resin.

Tall Pointy Prints

Prints that come to a narrow point (like the rocket in Figure 8-4) can be difficult to print because there is so little plastic being laid down that one layer does not cool before the next one starts. The Cura parameter Cooling ➤ Minimum Layer Time can help with this (make it a bigger number) but only so much, because the plastic will not cool very quickly when it is constantly in contact with the hot nozzle. A way to solve this problem is to also print a disposable object called a cooling tower to slow down the process. This gives the printer something to do while your plastic is cooling, rather than either simply slowing down but continuing to conduct heat from the hot nozzle or moving the nozzle into open air and letting it ooze. Figure 8-6 shows a print that comes to a point along with a cooling tower. Another option is to print more than one of an object at a time to give the nozzle more to do per layer. This print is the orbit of Halley's Comet, from our *3D Printed Science Projects* book (Apress, 2016).

Figure 8-6. *A print with a cooling tower*

Printing on Fabric

It is possible to print on fabric to get some interesting effects. David Shorey has been experimenting with printing a few layers on a platform, then layering fabric, then continuing the print. The result is in Figure 8-7, and the file is available at www.thingiverse.com/ShoreyDesigns/designs. Some printers may be challenging to use this way, because you need to be able to pause the print at a specified height and also clip down the fabric to the print bed in a way that does not interfere with the print.

Figure 8-7. *Cosplay dragon scales on fabric by David Shorey*

Printing Interlocking Pieces

You also may want to print chainmail or other interlocking parts. There are a lot of different chainmail designs out there on the various download sites if you want to experiment. Figure 8-8 shows an example designed by Rich in OpenSCAD. With care, these can be printed on a filament printer; fine-linked materials will need to be printed on a resin or powder (SLS) printer. There are service bureaus, like Shapeways, that will powder-print for you, but it is pricey.

Figure 8-8. *"Chainmail" printed in PETG*

If you create a design like this yourself on a filament printer, pay careful attention to maintaining clearances between pieces and avoid having features that fall below 1 mm or so, because they may not survive the printing process.

Printing Physically Big Objects

Consumer-level 3D printer build areas are, for the most part, relatively small, because it is a lot harder to manage temperature control and precision of the build platform and the rest of the machine's structure for a larger printer. As a result, most consumer printer build areas range somewhere between 100 and 300 mm in each dimension. This means that if you want to build something bigger than that, you are going to have to cut the object into pieces in software, print the parts, and then somehow construct the final object out of those pieces.

If you want to print an object that will not fit within the build volume, you can cut it into multiple pieces. For example, if the object is long and skinny, you can cut it into a few objects that you can then arrange on the build platform and print all at the same time. Otherwise, you will have to print the object using multiple runs. In either case, you will need to glue or assemble the piece afterwards.

Long Objects

If you have a long, skinny object that will not fit within the longest build dimension of your printer, first check to see whether it will fit diagonally on the platform. You will also want to keep the orientation that will minimize support, so there may be some tradeoffs there. If you are considering printing diagonally in all three dimensions, it may be easier to cut the object in half and later glue two pieces that would both lay flat rather than pick off a lot of support.

If you do need to print a thin but long object (for example, something shaped like a chopstick), you probably will be able to arrange the pieces on the platform next to each other and print them simultaneously. If, for instance, you were trying to print a tall, skinny tower, you could cut it into several pieces, lay out the pieces on the build platform in one or more groups, and then glue the pieces together. By selecting the right location to cut a model (for example, by cutting a model of a building between floors, or just below the edge of its roof), you may also be able to avoid supports that might otherwise be required.

Big Objects

If the object you are trying to print is too big in more than one dimension, you will need to split it along two axes—that is, into four or more pieces. If any parts require particular precision (if there will be critical joints, for instance), consider where your printer has the highest precision and arrange cuts so that those pieces will fall there.

It is tempting to use the surface that will be in contact with the print bed as your mating surface, because it needs to be flat anyway and will likely be much smoother than other surfaces. However, the first layer is often slightly over-compressed, which can result in excess plastic squeezed out around the edges and prints being slightly shorter than intended. The bottom also often comes out slightly warped, which may leave you with gaps between two parts when you try to glue them back together. This is particularly true of ABS prints, but even PLA can have this issue, especially when printed on a cold platform.

To avoid these issues, consider printing on a raft (see Chapter 3). This will protect against warping and allow any inconsistencies from the platform to even out before the printer begins on your model. Once the raft has been fully removed, this will likely leave you with a rougher surface than if you had printed without a raft. That surface texture, though, can actually give your glue more to hold on to, resulting in a stronger bond (though you may want to use a thicker glue than you would otherwise).

Even when the full part is too large in two or even three dimensions, it may be possible to divide it into just two or three pieces by judiciously cutting and then orienting the pieces. For example, a letter H that needs to be printed slightly larger than the build platform (in both x and y) can be cut into two halves, each of which may fit diagonally. A pyramid-shaped object that is too tall for the print volume and too wide only in one dimension may be cut into three pieces (the top and two halves of the base). An L-shaped object may be cut into four quadrants, one of which will be empty.

Be careful if your printer does not have consistent resolution throughout its build area. In most cases where resolution is variable, the best resolution is at the center of the print bed. A Cartesian printer should have consistent resolution across its build area, but deltas and machines with polar mechanisms usually do not. For resin printers, those using DLP projection or an LCD mask usually have consistent resolution, but may have differences in their light intensity near the edges. Those that use lasers typically direct them with galvanometers, which are a type of polar mechanism and thus can be variable.

Caution   The techniques discussed in the rest of this chapter are more similar to a "shop" environment (or a chemistry lab) than a computer lab environment. If you are not used to this type of environment, work with someone experienced first to learn safety procedures. Use eye protection and gloves, be sure your space is well ventilated, and follow the chemical manufacturer's instructions.

Gluing Pieces Together

Once you have printed the pieces, use glue that works on plastics. Cyanoacrylate adhesives ("superglues") work pretty well on PLA and ABS, though you will likely want to use the thicker gel style varieties to fill the gaps between layers if you want to glue to the side of a print (and especially if you want to glue to a surface that was slanted in the printing orientation). Nylon is difficult to glue with any adhesive appropriate for home use.

Caution   Before using any glue, read the manufacturer's instructions. Always use glues in well-ventilated areas. You may want to try out a particular glue on a few scrap pieces first to be sure that it does not discolor your material. Some glues may dissolve pieces a bit, which allows the "welding" process described later in this chapter.

Using an Acetone Slurry

If you are printing in ABS, there is another alternative for adhering pieces to one another (but see the Caution that follows). Acetone will melt ABS, so it can be used to weld one piece of ABS to another. Some people put a little bit of acetone in the type of bottle used for nail polish (ones with a small brush) and add the skirt, support material, or other scrap from the print.

The acetone will dissolve the scrap into a slurry that will weld the pieces together and fill the gaps created by layer lines without melting the edges of the print too much. Or, if precision edges are not important and your mating surfaces are sufficiently smooth, you can use a drop of acetone to bond the parts together. We talk about using acetone to smooth a print later in this chapter.

Caution   Acetone is flammable and volatile. Its vapor is invisible and heavier than air. The vapor can pool if you are in an unventilated area and cause a fire or explosion. Follow the cautions on the manufacturer's label.

Acetone welding only works for acetone-soluble plastics, such as ABS, MABS, or HIPS.

Caution   When you paint acetone on a part, the acetone evaporates, and you will get a bit of condensation from the air. This can make the surface of the object a bit cloudy.

Most other 3D-printing filament materials (such as PLA, nylon, and PET/PETG) are not acetone-soluble. Some PLA formulations (depending on additives) may partially melt, whereas others have been known to warp and crack when exposed to acetone.

Welding with a 3D Pen

One alternative to using chemicals and glues to weld parts together is to use a 3D pen (see Chapter 2) with the same filament as your print and weld prints together that way. It may not look very smooth but should be serviceable. Many people buy those pens just for this purpose.

Sanding, Painting, and Dyeing

All types of 3D printers will produce fine layer lines in printed objects, but the physics of filament-based printing tends to accentuate these lines more than other methods. You can think of them in one of two ways: as inherent in the medium (like brush marks on an oil painting) or as a problem that needs to be resolved.

If your application falls into the latter category, this section suggests some ways to get rid of those lines and to color your printed part other than by choosing colored filament. We talk about issues with chemical smoothing and then discuss sanding, painting, and dyeing finished prints.

Chemical Smoothing

There are various smoothing techniques described online that use acetone vapor to smooth ABS, along with do-it-yourself devices to create and handle the vapor. Many of these are unwise and/or too hazardous for the intended general audience of this book; therefore, none of these is described in this chapter. As of this writing, available solvents that can smooth most plastics other than ABS are too toxic to be used in a home or school environment.

Although we have not personally tried it, if you want to do a lot of vapor smoothing, you may want to look into Polysmooth's line of PLA-like filaments that are formulated to be smoothed with isopropyl alcohol vapor (using the Polysher vapor smoothing device, which it also sells). As always, be sure you are set up for the chemical handling the manufacturer suggests.

Sanding

A bit of sandpaper applied gently to PLA prints can significantly smooth the surface. Just use a piece of sandpaper and sand it by hand. Mechanical sanding, especially with a rotating drum like you would typically use with a rotary tool, is likely to melt the plastic.

Back at the beginning of the chapter (in Figure 8-1) we show PLA pieces that were hand-sanded with many grades of progressively finer sandpaper. A sanding block may also be useful, depending on the geometry of the part. Note that nylon just comes out worse than you started if you try sanding it.

Some plastics, particularly ABS, tend to whiten a bit when sanded, particularly those that bruise when bent. Wet sanding and continuing sanding with progressively finer grits may reduce this effect. For plastics that can be vapor smoothed, this chemical smoothing may reverse the discoloration, so sanding can be used in conjunction with vapor smoothing to reduce layer lines while maintaining sharper features that would be rounded off using vapor smoothing alone to remove the layer lines (though see the Caution above about acetone).

Painting and Clear Coats

You can paint ABS and PLA parts with acrylic paint, like that available in a typical hobby store. If you need a multi-color print and you have a one-extruder printer, painting the object after the fact is a good workaround to produce the colors you need.

There are clear coat products like XTC-3D that can be used to smooth a model by coating the surface (thereby filling in the layer lines) and that you may see suggested on user forums. Like other chemical methods, the manufacturers of these recommend personal protection that might not be available in a school or home environment; for example, see the recommendations at XTC's website, `www.smooth-on.com/product-line/xtc-3d/`. If you are planning to paint your model, using a high-build primer and/or a textured paint can also help to conceal layer lines.

Post-processing like this can lead to some spectacular results. *The Butterfrog* (Figure 8-9) by Vermont artist Rodney Batschelet was printed in three pieces. The wings were printed on their edges vertically and then glued to the body.

Figure 8-9. The Butterfrog *(Courtesy of the artist.)*

The frog is attached to the base using an old airbrush needle. Rodney tells us that the piece took about two hours of hands-on work: 5 minutes to coat all parts except the rock base with XTC-3D epoxy coating, an hour to prime all parts for final painting, 30 minutes to hand-paint basic colors with a brush, and about 10 minutes to add shading and rock color to the base with an airbrush.

The drying times during the process were also significant:

- *XTC-3D*: 2 hours

- *Primer*: 30 minutes

- *Hand-painted acrylic*: 30 minutes

- *Airbrush painting*: Dries immediately on contact

- *Goop glue*: About 30 minutes for each wing

Batschelet teaches at Benson Village School in Vermont and feels strongly that his students' 3D printed work needs to be finished (sanded, painted, and so on). He says that raw, unfinished prints look like toys, and he does not want his students to think of them that way in an art class. Figure 8-10 shows one of his students starting to paint an action figure she created.

Figure 8-10. *Student painting an action figure (courtesy of Rodney Batschelet)*

Dyeing Nylon

Although 3D printed nylon may not look the same as it does in fabric form, it will take up dye in a similar way. Nylon filament typically is white, which makes it easy to dye. People have had good luck with household cloth dyes when dyeing a printed nylon object; check the label on the dye package to be sure it works on nylon.

Resin Prints

Resin prints have extremely fine detail. "Resin" is a broad category of materials with a wide variety of chemical properties. As such, it is not really possible to talk broadly about what post-processing materials will work with a particular resin. Your printer manufacturer may have documentation on finishing on its website; you should see what is available to help you when you are looking into which printer to buy. Resins vary a lot in their properties, and some may be brittle and thus difficult to sand. You may need to experiment with your particular materials a little.

Casting and Jewelry-making

The *casting* process is very old, its origins lost in antiquity. It is still used today in many applications, from one-off casts through mass manufacturing. In brief, one creates a *pattern* in some material such as wood, clay, or wax (and in this chapter, PLA or resin). The pattern is a positive mold of what you want to cast in metal. Various techniques are used to pack sand or ceramic around the pattern. The pattern is then removed (*sand casting*) or melted away (*investment casting*), and metal fills the void where the pattern was.

Caution   The material in this chapter is intended to give you an idea about how an experienced artisan can create a metal piece based on your 3D print. It should give you enough information to create a part that will cast well. It is not a do-it-yourself guide to casting, though. You need to know more about safety procedures and equipment, which you should learn directly from an experienced artisan. We appreciate the insights of foundry artisan Peter Dippell.

Designing Models for Casting

This section gives some design rules for castable patterns, 3D printed or otherwise, in case you want to have someone cast a metal part from a print (pattern) that you make.

Sand Casting

The sand casting process is very old, as we mentioned, but it is still used today in many applications. A pattern is created (for example, by 3D printing) and then sand infused with a binder is packed around the pattern. Channels for pouring molten metal are carved into the mold, and the pattern is extracted. Molten metal is then poured into the empty space where the pattern was, and the final metal piece is extracted from the sand when it is cool enough.

Sand-cast patterns traditionally have been carved out of wood or another material that would survive the required number of uses. Because traditional patterns are used multiple times, being able to re-print them is not as much of an advantage as it is in investment casting. There, the pattern is lost each time (more on that in the next section). However, the channels needed to spread around the molten metal (called *sprues* and *runners*) need to be re-created each time in sand casting.

With careful thought (to avoid lots of support and other additional work), it may be possible to print these sprues and runners as well. Depending on your comfort with your chosen CAD program and its capabilities, it may or may not be easier for you to figure out how to make an STL file with the appropriate plumbing in addition to your main model. Bear in mind, too, that whoever casts your model will need to extract what you build from the sand, which could get tricky if you also want to avoid support.

For 3D prints that will be used for sand-casting, always use a bit of *draft*. That means that instead of having vertical surfaces intersect horizontal ones at right angles, surfaces that would have been vertical instead are tapered a bit to facilitate removal from the sand. In the case of the heart pendants in Figure 8-11, it would have helped to have a little bit of draft (just a few degrees) rather than the crisp verticals everywhere.

Figure 8-11. *Heart patterns and finished aluminum cast pieces*

Right angles can be printed by well-made 3D printers, but in sand casting the sand tends to get stuck in corners and edges and result in some imperfections. As you can see, the place where the vertical half-heart pokes upward is a little rough at its base because of the sharp edge there in the 3D printed version.

Tip   Engineering-style CAD programs (like Solidworks) have the ability to add draft to an object. It is difficult to do with beginner programs, however. If you are doing serious work that you want to be able to cast, you may need to step up to one of these more industrial-strength programs.

An *undercut* in the mold-making world is the equivalent of an *overhang* in 3D printing. It is a part of the model that (in this case) would pull out sand when the pattern is pulled out. Just as it is difficult for the printer to create an object that does not build up smoothly from the platform, it is hard to sand cast an object that cannot be pulled out of the mold smoothly. If a mold is made up of two pieces, those pieces also have to fit perfectly, with appropriate tolerances. As mentioned in the previous section, higher-end, engineering-oriented CAD programs have tools to separate parts for 3D printing and subsequent casting with the types of considerations noted here.

For the most part, it will be natural to print an object in the same orientation that you would cast it because many of the same considerations apply. However, objects tend to be strongest in the direction perpendicular to the layers, so an object may pull out of a mold best and be strongest if it is printed at 90 degrees from the orientation in which it would be cast. This may require more support and thus more scarring of the original 3D print, though, which would require cleanup before or after the casting. This 90-degree layer orientation may also be preferable because the x-y resolution of a print is typically much higher than the layer resolution (smoother detail can be produced on side surfaces than on top surfaces), and because the rounding of the edges of the layers creates a very tiny undercut between each layer and the previous one. Chapter 9 talks about functional prints.

Because metal contracts when it cools, your finished cast part will be smaller than your 3D printed part was. Be sure to account for this. You can look up the shrinkage (usually stated as a percentage) for your material and plan your 3D printed part to be a little bigger if your cast part needs to fit into something else precisely.

Think through *how* precisely parts need to fit together; do not make holes exactly the same size as the objects that need to fit into them. A little experimentation may be required to engineer your process end to end.

Tip   A manufacturing engineering textbook may be helpful to get a structured overview if metal casting and working with metal is new to you. One of the classics of the genre is *DeGarmo's Materials and Processes in Manufacturing* (Wiley, 2011) by DeGarmo, Black, and Khoser, with new editions appearing regularly.

Investment Casting

Sand casting is very versatile, but it is not good for capturing fine detail or for pieces that have complex geometries, such as a sculpture of a person. For that type of work, investment casting, sometimes called *lost-wax casting*, can be a good fit. With those advantages comes additional complexity. Investment casting has more steps and for high precision can take a lot longer than sand casting. Professional sculptors producing bronze statues typically use investment casting.

The process is pretty laborious, particularly if many copies are being made, because nothing survives the melt-out. First, a piece is carved in wax. Typically, sprues are also carved in advance and attached to the piece so that there are strategic paths to flow in metal and to allow air (and wax or, in our case, PLA) to escape. This wax piece is then coated with several layers of ceramic or plaster, or alternatively a plaster cast is made around it.

The plaster or ceramic is allowed to harden. The wax is "burned out" (melted away, hence the name *lost-wax*, since the pattern is lost each time), leaving the plaster cast. The hollow empty mold then is filled with metal. After it hardens and cools somewhat, the ceramic mold is broken open, and the piece is removed and cleaned up. 3D printing gives the option of printing the investment over and over, which might be a huge time-saver.

Wax has been used for the investment casting process for centuries because it burns out at a relatively low temperature and leaves a clean mold. As it happens, PLA has similar properties. Although the term has not yet entirely caught on, some people in the 3D-printing community have referred to using PLA in place of wax in lost-wax as a "lost-PLA" process. You cannot carve PLA, but you can definitely print multiple patterns to melt out. If you are seriously into this, you are probably better off using a resin printer that has a resin designed for the purpose. See the next section about the considerations there.

The sculpture in Figure 8-13 was created by Peter Dippell using a "lost-PLA" process starting with a 3D print very like the one in Figure 3-2. The subject was scanned with a 3D scanner (Chapter 3), which created an STL file (Chapters 3 and 6). The STL file was then converted into G-code (Chapter 3) and printed in PLA on a consumer-level printer. After that, it was pretty much the standard lost-wax process just described.

In Figure 8-12 you can still see the 3D printed layer lines. Whether this is a big problem or a charming reminder of where the piece was "born" is in the eye of the beholder. One can look at it as the "brush strokes" of a new medium. Alternatively, the piece could be sanded lightly before casting, or the piece could be polished at this point. However, sanding or polishing risks losing some of the very detail that investment casting seeks to preserve.

Figure 8-12. *An aluminum, investment-cast statue of Rich*

For those with a resin printer, there are resins specifically designed for lost-resin casting. Figure 8-13 shows a sample of castable resin and the resulting jewelry piece, courtesy of Formlabs. Resin prints are probably more suitable for jewelry, because of the better resolution achievable with resin. Curing the resin requires care, though. For example, Formlabs has detailed casting preparation instructions on its website (`www.formlabs.com`); browse the "Learn" section on the site for entries on jewelry.

Figure 8-13. *Castable resin and cast (model and photo courtesy of Formlabs)*

Low-Temperature Metals

Some metals and alloys have particularly low melting temperatures, allowing them to be cast in other types of molds. Some room-temperature-vulcanizing silicones can handle temperatures high enough to be used as a mold for casting pewter. Silicone is a popular material for mold making because its flexibility allows it to handle some geometries that would be a problem for sand casting, making it possible to create reusable molds for some shapes that would otherwise require investment casting.

Casting vs. Printing in Metal

Why not just print in metal in the first place? Printing in metal is expensive, although some research work is underway to make it less so. The commonest technique is to fuse a fine powder of metal, either using a binder or by selectively heating the particles enough to fuse them together. If a binder is used, it is typically removed in a post-processing step by heating the entire part. There is research going on at the moment to characterize how strong these materials are, predict when they are likely to fail, and so on. But these techniques are new, and it will take time to understand them fully.

Printing metal can also be dangerous. The fine metal particles used in these processes can be abrasive, extremely flammable, and explosive when dispersed in air; traditional casting has its own issues, but they are perhaps more obvious.

The advantages of taking a 3D print from a desktop filament printer and casting it traditionally are, first, the cost, and second, that it is a smaller step from existing processes. The second point is also a minus—it *is* a smaller step, and less of a dramatic breakthrough than pure metal printing will be once the issues are worked out. But in the meantime, it is a potentially cost-saving parallel option. You also need to take into account the surface finish smoothness you require and what the minimum-cost method is to achieve that.

Finding Casting Services

If you want to cast a part in metal, search for "metal casting" or "investment casting" and your city name in your favorite search engine. You can also see whether your local community college or high school has a jewelry design program; if it does, the program likely knows of a small-batch casting service or may offer the service for a fee itself. You can also talk to a shop teacher at your local high school or the people at a makerspace to find an artisan. Visiting a Maker Faire (`www.makerfaire.com`) is probably a good way to network, too.

Professional foundries may or may not be comfortable using PLA or resin in their investment casting workflow because it is not a medium they have used before and they may have evolved proprietary formulations they do not want to change. They may want to do the intermediary step of taking a mold from the 3D print and then burning out their wax as usual.

Note   If you want to create an STL file and print in metal in the first place, there are service bureaus that will create metal-printed parts for you. You can find a service bureau for printing in metal by searching for "3d printing metal services." Service bureaus that can print metal usually publish *design rules* that explain what they can and cannot do (including material properties, feature size, maximum part size, and so on). Some service bureaus also let you publish your design so others can print it.

Summary

This chapter reviewed some case studies of a variety of materials and geometries that might be particularly likely to arise in art and theater applications. We also went over ways to post-process prints and talked about some of the limitations. Finally, we discussed the best way to create 3D prints that are intended to be used as an intermediary product to ultimately create a metal cast part.

CHAPTER 9

Engineering, Math, and Science

It might seem that technology-focused teachers would be early adopters of 3D printing. However, particularly in high school, teachers in these subjects often feel they have too much to cover to add anything new. We think this is unfortunate, and that 3D printing has real power to offer alternative ways of learning beyond writing down notes from a whiteboard.

Typically, one of the bigger barriers to using a 3D printer is learning a CAD program. Schools with robotics or engineering programs often teach CAD already, so the students in those programs have a head start. Schools who are considering teaching coding could use OpenSCAD (Chapter 6) as a first language. OpenSCAD's language is similar to C, Python, Java, and other languages in the "C family," and is useful for scientific and math models.

No matter the CAD program used, though, creating good math or science models requires deep domain knowledge. Having students who need an extra challenge create models for their fellow students may be an option. We find we learn a lot whenever we dig into creating a model, because typically we have to go beyond textbooks and the 2D projections found in them. In this chapter, we share what we have learned about developing 3D printed math and science models. We also describe applications in robotics, and the issues that arise when you are creating functional parts.

© Joan Horvath, Rich Cameron 2018
J. Horvath and R. Cameron, *Mastering 3D Printing in the Classroom, Library, and Lab*,
https://doi.org/10.1007/978-1-4842-3501-0_9

Tip   We have written two books of science and math projects: *3D Printed Science Projects* (Apress, 2016) and *3D Printed Science Projects Volume 2* (Apress, 2017). The models are in OpenSCAD and are designed to be a middle ground between designing objects from zero and just downloading something prefabricated. Most of the models have parameters that can be changed to allow the student to explore what happens when the model changes, based on the science involved. The molecule, flower, and wing models we show as examples in this chapter (Figures 9-1 through 9-4) are described in the 2016 book.

Visualization

The most straightforward way to use a 3D print is to create a model of something that is inherently 3D, but perhaps not easy to handle normally—a molecule, for instance. Figure 9-1 shows a 3D model of an ice molecule. In Chapter 6 we discuss how to make models of molecules (in the "Specialized Databases" section).

Figure 9-1. *Ice crystal model (model from 3D Printed Science Projects)*

A first question to ask is whether the model you are considering creating really is inherently three-dimensional. We have seen people make flat 3D printed versions of diagrams. You can do that, but why? Other than the particular case of the visually impaired (described in Chapter 12), there is not a clear rationale, and the print will likely be harder to read than a traditional paper print. Even for the visually-impaired community, there are solutions for that sort of thing, like swell paper. For example, 3D printing a periodic table without adding any insights does not make a lot of sense, but there are a lot of periodic table models out there. On the other hand, adding another feature to the table for the third dimension might be interesting, like ones on www.thingiverse.com that use the third axis to show how properties of the elements like reactivity and density vary.

If a concept is abstract and naturally three-dimensional, as long as the relationships among the axes are correct and line up with the math, or physics, or what-have-you being described, a model can bring a lot of insight. Figuring out how to create the model is a learning experience, too, as you (or your students) wrestle with how to have the model's geometry show the concept you have in mind.

Experiments

Another good reason to make a model is to explore what happens if you start with a known system and vary some parameters. For example, we created a very simplistic model of plant growth in our 2016 *3D Printed Science Projects* book. Essentially, we assumed that plants lay out petals or leaves to minimize how much a leaf or a petal overlaps another. Then we made a few other assumptions about how many petals/leaves a plant would have and added some parameters that affected the shape of each leaf or petal. Figures 9-2 and 9-3 show models generated by the same design with different parameter values. The "aloe" generated by the program is shown next to its real equivalent in Figure 9-3.

Figure 9-2. *Flower growth model (photo and model from 3D Printed Science Projects)*

Figure 9-3. *Plant growth model and the real plant (photo and model from 3D Printed Science Projects)*

Another way to use 3D printing is to create an experimental setup. Figure 9-4 shows an airfoil model, also from our 2016 *3D Printed Science Projects* book. The model allows you to pick different wing cross-sections (airfoils) and to control how much the wing sweeps back and how much it tapers. Then the wing and a support are weighted down on a postal scale. When a fan is used to create a strong airflow over it, the wing will produce lift, and the reading on the scale will go down. If you have a 3D printer, this is a pretty cheap way to learn about wings and what the effects on lift are if the wing geometry changes.

Figure 9-4. *Airfoil model (photo and model from 3D Printed Science Projects)*

3D printing is also being used to create low-cost lab equipment. Scientists often are big consumers of duct tape, and 3D printing can create more opportunities to create one-off objects to hold things somehow. Of course, if there are chemicals involved, it becomes necessary to investigate whether or not the 3D printed materials involved are compatible with the chemicals in question. There are various open source science groups out there documenting their solutions, notably Joshua Pierce's group at Michigan Tech University. They maintain Appropedia (`www.appropedia.org/Open-source_Lab`), which has links to a variety of equipment, particularly for optics. Chapter 13 has more discussion on these topics.

Robotics

The international organization FIRST Robotics (For Inspiration and Recognition of Science and Technology, `www.firstinspires.org`) is which is making robotics a school sport, like basketball, with several leagues aimed at different age brackets. At the high school level, teams build robots that might weigh as much as 150 pounds. Many of them use 3D printing for a few components. Common applications are camera mounts and protective (and/or decorative) mounts or cases for small electronics.

Will Kalman coaches a FIRST high school team at Granada Hills Charter High School, the Robodox (Team 599, in FIRST parlance), which has been around for quite some time. When we asked him for an example of a good use of 3D printing, he told us about the part shown in Figures 9-5 and 9-6.

FIRST teams have to build a robot in six weeks and are eligible for awards if during the rest of the year they do community projects, demonstrate their robot at community events, and so on. Thus many teams have an "outreach bot" that may have been an earlier competition robot or could be a cannibalized Frankenstein of several earlier ones.

Currently, the Robodox use a previous year's robot as their outreach bot. This particular robot needed compressed air for some of its functions. They noticed when doing an outreach event that their air compressor was overheating because they were using it so heavily. It actually got hot enough that it softened a plastic air hose, which subsequently blew out.

The team decided to add a fan to cool the air compressor to avoid having that happen again. Team member Omeed Shahhosseini designed and implemented the fix shown in Figures 9-5 and 9-6. The new part takes air from a fan and turns the air so that it blows on the compressor to keep it cool. The part also had to fit onto a chassis rail to keep this ductwork oriented correctly and had to be sturdy enough to support the forces involved.

The resulting overall design (Figure 9-5) supports a fan (Figure 9-6) and turns the air from the fan (in the foreground of Figure 9-5) back around to cool the compressor connector, under the domed part in Figure 9-5. It has solved the problem nicely.

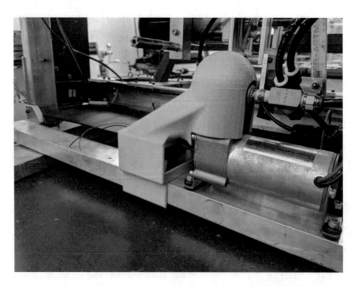

Figure 9-5. *Fan and ducting (model by Omeed Shahhosseini, photo by Will Kalman)*

Figure 9-6. *Closeup of fan housing (model by Omeed Shahhosseini, photo by Will Kalman)*

Functional Parts

As with the robotics applications we just saw, sometimes a *functional part* is required—that is, a part that is not just a decorative, standalone piece but one that is part of a bigger project or that is doing something that requires at least some mechanical strength. We know that once students learn a CAD program that can also model forces, they tend to rely on it and believe that if it says a part is strong enough, it is.

However, for 3D printing that can be tricky. For printing with filament, the strength of parts varies a lot based on the manufacturer and variability in the qualities of the filament itself. Some manufacturers now quote strength parameters, but this tends to be based on expensive, specialty filament, typically tested after a tightly controlled printing process of a standard simple part.

People are beginning to attempt to define standards, and there are papers being written on the strength of 3D prints. Appropedia and open-access journal articles it references are a good free source of information to get started, at `www.appropedia.org/Tensile_Strength_of_Commercial_Polymer_Materials_for_Fused_Filament_Fabrication_3-D_Printing`.

But even if you do have nominal numbers for the strength of a filament and data from other people's tests, the temperatures used for printing, specifics of the printer, the settings you are using, and the geometry and orientation of the print itself all matter too. As we saw in the "Shells" section of Chapter 3, your slicer will allow you to specify the thickness of the horizontal shell, either as a number of perimeters or in millimeters (which will be rounded to a multiple of your perimeter extrusion width). Two is typically a good number.

The width (in the *x-y* plane) of this perimeter is the extrusion width, which must be no smaller than your nozzle diameter, and might be larger. For a given extrusion width, if you are using thick layers the interlayer adhesion might not be as good as it would be if you used thin layers, which will be more compressed and have more contact area. If the nozzle temperature is too low, that can lead to worse interlayer adhesion.

The bottom line is that prints will be stronger *within* a layer than *across* layers, in a way that is not entirely predictable. This is called *anisotropy*, meaning that the material has different properties in different directions. You can think of it as the grain in wood, which makes it break more easily in some directions than others. A specific example may help show why this is true. Figure 9-7 shows a motor mount printed in three orientations. It would be used to hold a motor in the round hole with four screws, and then attach the motor to a wall or other surface with the part at right angles that has two holes in it. In what follows, we call the part with the two holes the "base."

Figure 9-7. *Motor mount printed in three orientations*

Look carefully at Figure 9-7. Which one of these three parts would you expect to be the strongest and least likely to fail during its intended use? Where are the inter-layer lines?

Caution   This part has been created to be too flimsy for its intended purpose so that we could make a point. It was printed in PLA, with the temperature deliberately a little too low to make this a more spectacular demo.

First consider the part on the upper left in Figure 9-7, printed upright with the base down. We might be concerned that this print might snap along the line between the base and the rest of the mount, since a layer line runs along the top of the base. It also has some unsupported overhangs, although all of them are small or climb at less than 45 degrees, so do not need support. When the print is flexed to destruction (by holding it in two hands and flexing it), it snaps easily at that point, as shown in Figure 9-8. Indeed, when we create a set of these motor mounts for demonstrations, we have to be careful not to break it just getting it off the platform.

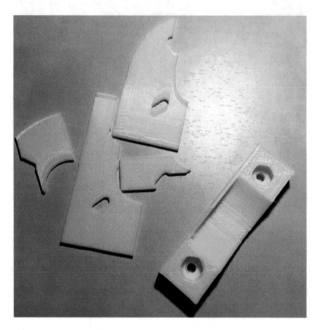

Figure 9-8. *Motor mount printed vertically, base down*

Next, consider the print flat on the platform in Figure 9-7, with the base poking up. In earlier chapters we advised printing exactly like that—a nice, big base area, and minor acceptable overhangs. But Figure 9-9 shows that this, too, had one layer line between the base and the rest of the mount. This makes it very vulnerable to a critical failure, even if it is pretty strong within the part that was flat on the platform (which took much more force to break).

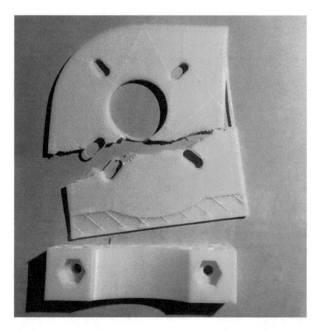

Figure 9-9. *Motor mount printed flat on the plaform, base sticking up*

Finally, consider the print on the upper right of Figure 9-7, printed vertically with an L-shaped layer all the way up. This one is very strong—sometimes it is almost impossible to break it. It tends to also break in a way that might allow it to function for a while even after it broke (Figure 9-10).

Figure 9-10. *Motor mount printed on its side, layer lines perpendicular to base*

These parts were all printed in PLA, so if the motor they were holding got hot (or if we left them on a hot car dashboard in summer), they would warp. UV radiation degrades many plastics, too.

So, what to do? The simplest thing, particularly in a K-12 environment, is to thoroughly test the part before using it for something load-bearing. Consider how hot it will get, whether it will be outside for a long period of time, and so on. Constructing the tests and interpreting the results can be a good project in and of itself, and lends itself to an age-appropriate level. (Of course, if you are going to break things, use eye protection and protect the hands of the person breaking the part.)

Note   Resin prints are more homogeneous than filament-based ones but have their own issues. Resin part strength is critically dependent on following the appropriate post-cure processes, and even then standard resins can be very brittle.

If the exercise of making a functional part is embedded in an engineering class, it is also an opportunity to discuss what to do when the CAD software cannot be completely trusted. We have seen students get upset when a part that "should have been strong enough" (according to the CAD program) snapped instead. Thinking about why this happened and the need to use judgment in addition to software tools might be a memorable lesson. At least, it makes a different point than seeing a lot of parts that *did* work, but maybe only because the designer got lucky. Chapter 2 has more discussion of materials' properties to help you think about a good choice given your printer's capabilities.

Conductive Parts

If you have a printer that can lay down two materials at a time, you may be tempted to use conductive filaments to lay down conductive paths in your part. These filaments are made of PLA or another material with embedded graphite; this makes the filament somewhat abrasive for your nozzle. The graphite makes them mildly conductive, but the resistance can be pretty high. So, if you are trying to carry current—say, to light an LED—its ability to carry enough current might be a little marginal.

Filament manufacturer Proto-pasta, for instance, quotes a volume resistivity for its conductive PLA of 3D printed parts along layers of 30 ohm-cm and across layers of 115 ohm-cm (www.proto-pasta.com/collections/exotic-composite-pla/products/conductive-pla). Note that the ohm-cm units indicate that the resistance will be lower if the cross-sectional area of the conductive part of the print is bigger, and lower if the distance current has to travel through the print get smaller. The resistance is proportional to the cross-sectional area divided by that distance. However, if you have an application that does not require a lot of current, such as creating capacitive touch sensors, printing a conductive trace might allow you to create some interesting circuitry embedded in a housing. You could be better off, though, just leaving room to run wire or another conductive material through a gap in your print.

Tip   If you are developing Arduino electronics for a robot or similar project, you can make housings in Tinkercad. Tinkercad now has the ability to simulate a circuit and help you design enclosures around certain electronic components (`www.tinkercad.com/circuits`).

Learning More

The key to using 3D printing effectively in a science or math context is to solve a problem that needs solving. This means it is best to guide the choice of problem for students (or for faculty wanting models) based on math or science needs. This sounds obvious, but for some reason people often start with the tool and try to find an application for it. Try asking yourself, "What would I love to have my students make (or make for my students) that just does not seem possible?" Then see if 3D printing (or another maker technology) can get you partway there.

The recent boom in citizen science projects, where the public participates in real scientific endeavors, may be the next frontier for 3D printing. Currently, most of these projects, like those at `www.zooniverse.org`, are focused on having the public take or interpret images. But we and others have been trying to help scientists think about having people take data for them in other ways, perhaps involving creating DIY instrumentation plans that someone can download and print. There are issues there to be sure (standardization, for one) that need to be worked out, but in principle it might be an exciting new area for citizen science.

We are particularly interested in finding ways to teach math differently using the types of model we talk about in this chapter. You can check out our Hacker Calculus project, which is reimagining calculus teaching by taking advantage of 3D prints, at `https://hackaday.io/project/20621-hacker-calculus`.

We have also been inspired by Paul Lockhart's book *A Mathematician's Lament* (Belleview Literary Press, 2009). Written by a mathematician who teaches at the high school level, the book discusses how to teach math intuitively. He has several other books, too, about ways of teaching math with less notation and more understanding.

Summary

In this chapter, we discussed how to use 3D printing to create math and science visualizations, and to enable experimentation. Robotics teams and engineering classes can use the technology to solve real-world problems, and to discover the limits of modeling and prediction for materials that are not the same throughout a part. Specialty filaments, like conductive ones, might open other experiment opportunities. Finally, we noted that 3D printing and other maker technologies can open up new opportunities for teachers, students, and other members of the public to take part in real scientific explorations.

CHAPTER 10

Language Arts and Social Studies

People often ask us how to use 3D printers outside of obvious areas like robotics and art. Some of the most creative applications we have seen, actually, have been in disciplines that lend themselves to storytelling. We all made dioramas with cardboard in middle school, but we can now go beyond that.

One concern that we know teachers have is that they do not want to spend a lot of class time in history, literature, and similar subjects teaching students how to use a 3D printer (or learning how to do it themselves). Schools have addressed this situation in several ways. Students who are interested can learn how to prepare a file for 3D printing themselves during lunch or after school time, or a small group of students may become "designated users." In other cases, a staff person is in charge of actual printing, and students just create the computer model.

Regardless of the level of student (and teacher) training, creating a model that tells a story is not as easy as it sounds. Thinking about the model conceptually and then implementing will cause students to think about what they are modeling differently than they would if they were writing a paper about the topic. Tinkercad (particularly now with its "Scribble" function that enables freehand drawing) is a perfectly adequate tool for most of the explorations we describe in this chapter.

J. Horvath and R. Cameron, *Mastering 3D Printing in the Classroom, Library, and Lab*, https://doi.org/10.1007/978-1-4842-3501-0_10

Models That Tell a Story

Illustrating a key point from a story (whether in the context of teaching history or literature) means you have to think about what is critical in the story and visualize it yourself first. Picking out what story to tell (and scoping it so that it is a plausible project) can make students think hard about the story.

Obviously, if students have open-ended requests to develop a model about key events of the French Revolution, some will make articulated guillotines and some will try to make models of Versailles. Either way, significant background research and iteration will be required.

One option that 3D printing opens up for historical discussions is the possibility of being able to look at accurate 3D terrain of an area where an event took place. The next section discusses how to print terrain representing anyplace on the Earth or moon. Looking at migrations, battles, or even just US westward expansion may be interesting options for looking at terrain more realistically than is possible with just topographical maps.

Tip   Every school and library 3D-printing facility needs to think about whether or not to allow the printing of human-scale historical or sci-fi/fantasy weaponry. There are obvious safety issues with allowing students or patrons to print functional weapons, or even realistic replicas. On the other hand, most would allow printing a 4-inch high toy soldier. It gets a little blurrier for theatrical props or history projects. Think through a clear policy and be sure faculty and students know about it.

Creating Terrain

Creating 3D terrain is a powerful application of 3D printing for geography, history, and other applications. At some level, you can accomplish the same insight from a topographical map, but we have found that having an actual 3D model of a mountain range or varied terrain like the Los Angeles basin makes it much easier to see large-scale geology and also to imagine the sweep of historical events taking place on the landscape.

A wonderful free program that lets you print anyplace on Earth is Thatcher Chamberlain's Terrain2STL, at `http://jthatch.com/Terrain2STL/`. An equivalent program for the moon can be found at `http://jthatch.com/Moon2STL/`. The program creates an STL file of an arbitrary-sized area and allows you to exaggerate the vertical. Vertical exaggeration is useful not only to accentuate terrain features, but also because the print's layering is less obvious on the steeper surfaces that it creates, and subtler features may be lost entirely if they are less than one layer high.

Without vertical exaggeration, you will likely find that the print quality is better if you rotate the models to print vertically. Oriented this way, only the most extreme terrain features will produce unprintable overhangs, and the printer will be able to reproduce much finer variations in elevation.

Figure 10-1 is a print of the area around Pasadena, California, with a vertical exaggeration of around ten times, making the San Gabriel Mountains and their floodplain clearly visible. If you want more vertical exaggeration than the program offers, you can always do more in your printer's slicing software, which usually will let you scale in just one axis.

Figure 10-2 shows the area around Mt. Whitney in California with no vertical exaggeration (the valley floor is at about 4000 feet, and the mountain peak is 14,000) The Mt. Whitney print was printed vertically.

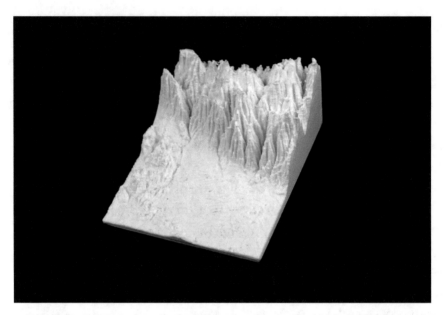

Figure 10-1. *Pasadena terrain model created by Terrain2STL, high vertical exaggertion, printed flat (as shown)*

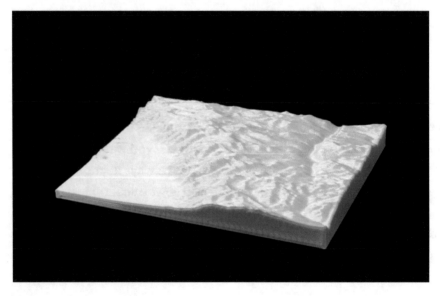

Figure 10-2. *Mt. Whitney area, no vertical exaggeration, printed vertically*

Terrain model files can get too large for slicing programs to handle easily, and cleaning them up a little can be handy. Doing so might lose some fine detail, but it makes them easier to use in other programs later. To fix problems with STL files (called *meshes* in other software), we often use the open source, free program Meshlab. Meshlab is not the friendliest program on earth, but it does work well. You can download it from `www.meshlab.net`.

To reduce the size of an STL file in Meshlab, first import the mesh (STL file) into Meshlab. Then go to the menu and select Filters ➤ Remeshing, Simplification and Construction ➤ Quadratic Edge Collapse Decimation. Cut the number of triangles by 50% (enter **0.5** in the dialog box) as a first approximation. If that's too much, do not save your file (it will overwrite the original as a default) but instead load it in again and try a less aggressive adjustment.

If a model just looks funny in your slicing software, open it in Meshlab, accept any suggestions the program makes, and export it to try again in your slicing software.

If you want to model a large area, you can carefully make adjacent sections in software and print them out in pieces. There are also software tools that will let you cut an STL into parts, including Autodesk Meshmixer (`www.meshmixer.com`).

Tip   If you are interested in geologic features beyond just printing terrain, see the geology models in our book *3D Printed Science Projects Volume 2* (Apress, 2017).

Examples of Student Projects

Many have fond memories (or not) of making a shoebox diorama at some point. It is not big step to imagine making 3D printed pieces to include in a traditional diorama that is otherwise made with craft materials. If part of the point of an assignment is to have students learn some digital manufacturing techniques across the curriculum, one option is always to require that some part of a traditional diorama-type assignment be constructed that way.

A discussion of Tinkercad or a similar program and design rules for 3D printing (both in Chapter 6) is probably enough to get students started for something like this. In our experience, most schools and libraries have a staff person slice and print the file, although some high schools have programs that train self-selecting students to own that process.

3D Vermont

The 3D Vermont competition (`http://3dvermont.org`) has been organized for several years by a high school teacher, who has since received support from backers including Preservation Trust of Vermont, Vermont's Agency of Education, the Vermont Department of Housing and Community Development, Division of Historic Preservation, and others listed on the site.

Students create a model of a building of historical interest with supporting information and then gather together to present their model and discuss its importance, and to place it in the appropriate spot on a giant model of the state of Vermont. Rules are written up on the site, and prizes are involved.

If you want to see some examples of the competition, look on Twitter (`twitter.com`) for posts with the hashtag #3dVermont. Clearly this works best in a region (like Vermont) where it is plausible for students to travel to get together and compete, but one could imagine more local variations.

As an aside, if you are thinking about starting a modest competition of your own, we would at this point suggest standardizing on Tinkercad rather than Sketchup. Sketchup is intended as an architectural tool and so makes sense from that perspective, but it is notorious for making models that have printing issues because it was not primarily designed for the purpose. There is more on this in Chapter 6.

The Silk Road

Crossroads School in Santa Monica, California, is a creative user of maker technologies. We visited with Dori Friedman, middle school EdTech and MakerEd coordinator, to see what sorts of projects were working well. We appreciate the time Friedman spent with us and Crossroads' permission to use photos of student projects in this book.

One that caught our eye was a project in which students were asked to come up with a game that would teach them about trade along the Silk Road, the ancient trade route between Europe and Asia. 3D printing was used to make game pieces and parts of the boards (Figures 10-3 and 10-4). Games were displayed in a glass case in the hallway after they had served their purpose.

Figure 10-3. *Silk Road game designed by Crossroads School students*

Figure 10-4. *Detail of Silk Road game in Figure 10-3 (game by Crossroads School students)*

Vikings and 3D Pens

Crossroads students were learning about Vikings in their Core courses, which are a combination of English and History. Friedman decided to have them make Viking ships with 3D pens as a big group.

Note   3D pens are discussed in Chapter 8 in the context of welding a broken print; this is an interesting application of using them to create novel designs.

First Friedman designed and created 3D prototype versions of the ships, shown hanging on the wall Figure 10-5. The lowest model in Figure 10-5 is a 3D version of the school logo.

Next she laid out a pattern for the ship, shown in Figure 10-6, which is one of a few ships, each several feet long. Students worked with 3D pens to fill in the diagram. Finally, she (carefully!) lifted the fragile ships up and hung them high on the wall around their makerspace.

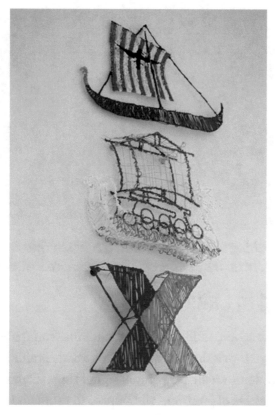

Figure 10-5. *Two 3D Viking ships and the Crossroads logo created with a 3D pen (models by Dori Friedman)*

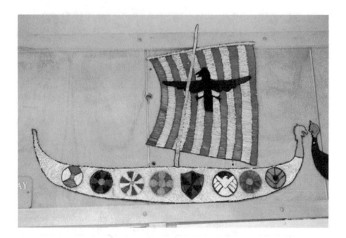

Figure 10-6. *Viking ship created with a 3D pen (model template by Dori Friedman, artwork completed by Crossroads students)*

3D Printing in Latin Class

Not all that many schools still offer Latin, and one would not expect it to be fertile ground for 3D printing. However, Crossroads Middle School Latin teachers had students create 3D printed signet rings (Figure 10-7). The students wrote letters of gratitude, in Latin, to the staff and sealed them with their 3D printed signet rings (Figure 10-8).

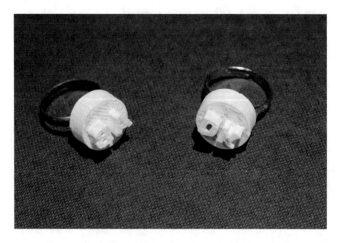

Figure 10-7. *Crossroads School signet rings (Figure 10-7). The students.*

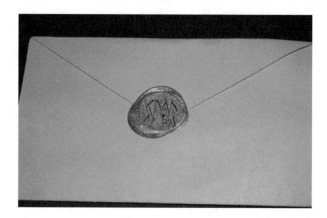

Figure 10-8. *Wax seal closed with a ring, from the Crossroad signet ring (Figure 10-7). The students project.*

Signet rings (Figure 10-7). The students historically were used as signatures, to enclose a document with a tamper-evident seal. Thus this project involved a bit of history, Latin, and perhaps the opportunity for a sidebar on document security, all in one relatively simple print.

Summary

3D printing can be a curriculum enhancer in a variety of subjects, sometimes in ways that are not very complex to design. This chapter touched on projects in language arts, social studies, and similar fields to show how some innovative educators are using 3D printing and related technologies to make these subjects come alive for students. We also discussed how to create 3D terrain models of any place on earth (or the moon!) relatively easily to enable teaching of history, geography, and other subjects.

CHAPTER 11

Elementary Students

We are frequently asked what a makerspace in an elementary school should do and what equipment it can include. Elementary students have always made things, and just as the ability to make a typed report has migrated younger, so too can professional-looking art pieces. What makes sense will largely depend on the school style, budget, and similar factors that are not universal. In this chapter, we give you some anecdotal information and resources developed by early adopters.

Chapters 8 and 10 give you some ideas that might work for younger students. What we will focus on in this brief chapter are some special considerations for younger students and makerspaces that serve them, and their use of 3D printing in particular.

What Is Realistic?

There are four hurdles to a successful 3D print. You need to figure out what you are trying to make. Then you need to create the CAD file and figure out the slicing settings and print orientation. Finally, you will manage the actual printing process and any post-processing. Typically, elementary students will only go to the point of creating a CAD file, although in Chapter 8 you can read about examples of students painting prints.

Most 3D printers are designed primarily for the adult market, or at least are recommended for age 13 and over. Generally speaking, this feels about right to us. Most schools designate a staff person, a teacher, or (if they have one) a makerspace manager to deal with the equipment. In some cases this falls to the school librarian. If the school is K-12, though, older students may be able to undergo some extra training and earn a defined role in a makerspace—perhaps managing the queue of jobs to 3D printers, doing quality control on CAD files, or slicing the files.

Another thing to consider is whether 3D prints can be part of a larger fabrication project. Maybe a project is mostly cardboard, but a decorative or functional part is made with a 3D printer. Having students think about what tool to use for what job is a key part of the real-life design process, but too often we see teachers trying to find a reason to use a 3D printer and constructing an artificial project. It is better, if possible, to let an organic design need create a use case for a 3D printer (or any tool).

The right project prompt is important, too. It should be neither too specific nor so broad that students do not know where to start. This is a natural way to fit design into other subjects (for example, illustrating part of a story, or solving a problem a character encounters in a story). Chapter 7 looks at these issues for teachers generally, and you may find some further insights there.

Tip   If you are interested in reading blogs with real stories of life in educational making, particularly for the younger set, you might enjoy Lucie deLaBruere's journal, at `http://createmakelearn.blogspot.com`. Lucie often collaborates with Rodney Batschelet, whose work you can read about and see in Chapter 8 (we appreciate their suggestions). John Umekubo's eponymous website, `https://johnumekubo.com`, is another elementary-focused source of maker-educator news and practical ideas.

Design

The maker movement has resulted in the democratization of CAD tools, discussed in depth in Chapter 6. Tinkercad (`www.tinkercad.com`) and Morphi (`www.morphiapp.com`) are common choices for the younger set. Tinkercad has the virtue and problem that it is entirely web based, but it is free and always adding new features. Morphi is a downloadable app, available at a modest price per student.

Younger students, though, tend to make unprintable designs in Tinkercad. Often, they will have pieces of "one part" hovering over one another or poking below the level of the platform. A discussion of basic design constraints, at an age-appropriate level, can help. (Have a large, flat base, avoid overhangs, be sure features are not too small, and so on.) We have found that pictures of "the right way" to design something for 3D printing (or any fabrication technology), along with what happens when things are created "the wrong way," to be valuable to learners of all ages.

Tinkercad used to operate purely by dragging, dropping, and adding and subtracting prefabricated shapes, but it has now added a "Scribble" function. This allows you to do a limited amount of freehand drawing, such as Joan's name on the side of the roof in Figure 11-1, and add these freehand parts to other shapes.

Even if young students do not have access to a 3D printer, learning CAD programs early will give them a head start later on if they do have access to digital fabrication tools when they are older.

Figure 11-1. *Demonstration of the Scribble functionality in Tinkercad*

Tip   If you are running the makerspace, you will want to come up
with a policy about what acceptable use of school 3D printers is.
Classwork only? If not, do teachers give permission? Are they only
allowed to print their own designs, or can they pull down things from
Thingiverse and print them (or have them printed)? Who pays for
filament? We talk about these issues more in Chapter 7. In an ideal
world, teachers will want to make prints to demonstrate concepts,
and priorities will need to be set up.

Teaching Coding

Teaching CAD can be part of teaching coding. Tinkercad has recently
added Codeblocks, which are based on Scratch blocks. This feature, in beta
as of this writing, is a way to tie in coding and design.

At a more sophisticated level, OpenSCAD (also discussed in Chapter 6) enables you to develop models based on code rather than drag-and-drop objects. It may not be appropriate for the average elementary student, however; it is a C-like language (a family of languages that also includes Java and Python) and requires being able to handle coding at that level.

Summary

Elementary-level students will most likely be involved in the front end of the 3D printing process (design and CAD) and possibly in the post-processing (painting). In-between there will likely be a need for some support for slicing and running the prints, and for other steps that may need more grown-up equipment. Using the design process as training for later hands-on work might be a realistic way to go, too.

CHAPTER 12

The Special-Needs Student

Special-needs teachers always have to be creative and often must invent props to get their points across. 3D printing can have a particular role to play for learners who benefit from tactile interactions.

However, as we have seen in Chapter 6 and elsewhere, creating effective models can be challenging. Models from free databases can be hard to print, or may represent the concept they claim to show incorrectly or incompletely. Models for math and science, in particular, often need some background materials with the model so that the assumptions and constraints are clear.

In this chapter, we focus on educational models—models that a teacher or parent might use to get across a concept. There are, of course, professionals using 3D printing in a variety of medical applications. There are also amateur groups attempting to create customized designs to assist people with daily living. Some of these are created through contests and hackathons, and others through organized, ongoing programs.

Traditional nonprofit disabled advocacy groups are also getting involved. The Neil Squire Society in Canada (`www.neilsquire.ca`), for example, has a Makers Making Change initiative that brings together hobbyist inventors and people who need a problem solved.

© Joan Horvath, Rich Cameron 2018
J. Horvath and R. Cameron, *Mastering 3D Printing in the Classroom, Library, and Lab*,
https://doi.org/10.1007/978-1-4842-3501-0_12

Teaching the Visually Impaired

One of the most obvious applications of 3D printing is in teaching the blind or visually impaired, although creating these models often requires more thought than anticipated.

Making Tactile Models

A model that is an accurate representation of a fundamentally 3D shape can avoid the type of problem shown in Figures 12-1 and 12-2. In these figures, we printed an actual cube and a classic perspective drawing of a cube.

***Figure 12-1.** An actual cube and a perspective drawing print of one*

Making a raised-line drawing of existing book figures is a common way of making a textbook accessible. As you can see in Figure 12-2, though, for a geometrical object such as a cube, a 3D representation is far more useful. This is the same pair of objects as in Figure 12-1, but as you can see, the perspective print is pretty counterintuitive viewed from the wrong angle. A blind student (who does not routinely see the world as a 2D projection with perspective the way a sighted person does) may find it misleading at best. As a blind friend of ours noted, though, it might be useful if you are specifically teaching a blind person about perspective.

Figure 12-2. *Showing the reality of the perspective "cube" from another angle*

A lot of subtle issues are involved in developing good tactile models. Do you want Braille labels, and if so how do you make it clear that something is a label and not a feature? What is a comfortable scale for a model, and how much detail should you keep? What is the minimum feature size someone can feel, and how does that relate to the best your particular printer can produce? If you are collecting a database of validated models, what are good criteria for selection? Can models really stand alone, or do they need extensive background materials to be "classroom worthy"?

We and others are involved in trying to create some guidelines. Standards get unwieldy if they are too detailed, but can leave too much to the imagination if they are not detailed enough. Various groups around the world are attacking these challenging issues.

Note   Your authors became interested in the issues of making
3D printed models for educators some time ago and have found
ourselves involved in helping to come up with standards for tactile
models. We are both members of the 3D Tactile Standards Working
Group, currently chaired by Jim Allan of the Texas School for the Blind
and Visually Impaired (TSVBI). This is a working group of the DIAGRAM
(Digital Image and Graphic Resources for Accessible Materials) Center.
DIAGRAM is an initiative of Benetech, a California nonprofit, and
several partners and sponsors. If you are interested, see the resources
collected at `http://diagramcenter.org/3d-printing.html`.

One thing we have discovered in the course of thinking about blind
student users is that models that are useful for them tend to be useful for
students generally. For example, learning about the relative volumes of
different simple geometrical shapes is challenging for blind students, but
really, that is true for everyone. In architecture, this philosophy is known as
universal design, and the general principles apply here.

Case Study: Constant-Volume Models

Rich designed a set of hollow geometrical shape models (Figure 12-3) that
all have the same internal volume. The intent is that you can pour water
from one to another and prove to yourself that these geometries indeed
hold the same amount of water. He put them out on Youmagine as an
open source, freely available set of models (available at `www.youmagine.`
`com/designs/fixed-volume-objects`). The little balls on top of the taller
models, added at the request of a teacher, make the models less pointy for
blind children's use. This modification also has the side effect of making
them easier to print, because a point is difficult to print reliably. (This is a
good example of how easy it is in 3D printing to modify designs on the fly.)

We have been surprised by how popular these models have been. We have found that almost no adults remember that a cone has the same volume as a cylinder one-third as tall with the same-diameter base; this also applies pyramids and prisms with any number of sides, so long as the base area remains constant. The models are very good for impromptu geometry refreshers—and for letting kids who just learned about that to feel very superior to Mom or Dad. Our takeaways from this experience included the following:

- Simple is good.

- We decided Braille labels would be fussy and distracting and did not use any.

- Attention to detail and use cases are important. (As mentioned, students may hurt themselves on a pointy model, especially blind students, who cannot see where the point is before they touch it and may reach for it too quickly).

- The "storytelling" of the model is critical and may evolve as you use it in teaching. For example, it works a lot better if you have three of the short models to show that the cone is three times the height of the cylinder.

- Models should be conducive to "experiments"—in this case, stacking the models, comparing their bases (the base areas are the same), filling them with water or sand to test out the volume relationships, and so on.

- Models need to be technically correct. In this case, the internal volume had to be the same, which required some care and knowledge of how the 3D printer was going to lay up material. CAD programs design outer surfaces more easily than internal ones. In other words, it helps to have intimate knowledge of how a 3D printer will produce the model.

- Models should print easily on the poorly tuned and somewhat abused 3D printers found in schools, and not require too much teacher fiddling with settings.

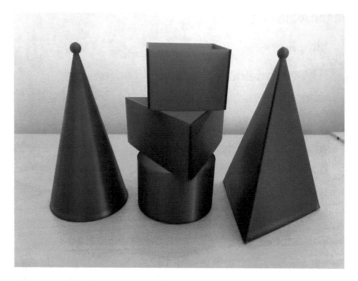

Figure 12-3. *Constant-volume models*

3D Printed Braille

One final challenge is deciding whether and how to add Braille to a print. Braille has a standard size and dot shape. Unfortunately, these dots are small enough to be dicey to print. Figure 12-4 shows Braille printed in three orientations.

Caution   Braille has very specific size constraints, so you need to scale your print correctly before adding Braille to it. Otherwise you may end up with labels that are at best hard to read.

One might naturally try to print Braille on the top surface of a print, but as you can see in Figure 12-4, the print layering will result in rough dots that are uncomfortable to read, and that likely have stringing between them. Also, as we discuss in Chapter 9, prints are stronger within a layer than between them. Braille printed on a top surface of a print is prone to being rubbed off. Our conclusion after some experimentation is that it is best to print Braille on the vertical sides of a print, to get maximum resolution and strength.

Figure 12-4. *3D printed Braille in three orientations*

Tip   Rich developed an OpenSCAD program to print standard individual Braille letters (it we used it to create the letters in Figure 12-4). It is available at `https://github.com/whosawhatsis/braille-openscad`.

TVI Challenges

In the end, the biggest challenge for extensive use of 3D printing for teaching these students has been that teachers of the visually impaired (TVIs) are often itinerant, travelling from school to school to meet with their students. They have very little time to learn to use a printer, and are hampered in printing things themselves because they are often at different schools on subsequent days.

Designing models is harder than it looks, too; there is more on this in Chapter 6. We created a Google Group, called 3D Printed Education Models where TVIs can post requests for models they would like to have, at `https://groups.google.com/forum/#!forum/3dp_edu_models`. The idea is that teachers at schools with makerspaces who could not think of projects could fulfill these requests and put the results up as open source, as we did with the constant-volume models. As of this writing, we have many more requests than attempts to fulfill them, but we hope this will be a future inspiration for students looking for a good project.

There have been various other attempts at similar matchups, including a hackathon by Benetech and community calls by others, but progress remains slow. We hope that our books of 3D printed science and math projects are making a dent in this void. We would like to acknowledge TVIs Lori Schindler, Yue-Ting Siu, Michael Cheverie, Jim Allan, and Sue O'Brien for technical suggestions and inspiration, and Lindsay Yazzolino for model design feedback.

Tip   A 3D pen (described in a sidebar in Chapter 2 and in the "Vikings and 3D Pens" example in Chapter 10) might be useful for quick-and-dirty models of simple objects. But models tend to be fragile, and we are not sure how practical a 3D pen may be for any multi-use model.

Learning Differently

What about using 3D prints for other students who need to learn differently? For students who learn best by assembling or making things, a 3D printed model can be a game changer. The two of us, for example, learn and think very differently, and we have found that the process of creating models and talking about how to use them makes us both learn a lot more than we might otherwise. Joan learns reasonably well by reading books or going to traditional lectures, but Rich does much better if he can create a 3D model and manipulate it, even if only on a screen.

To this point, we have largely talked about teachers creating or finding models. For visually impaired students, the CAD options are limited (OpenSCAD has a command-line interface that is somewhat accessible). But for students with other learning differences who can use CAD, perhaps there are creative ways to use model design to engage students and get across content.

Tip   Although not a 3D printing or special ed book per se, Joan found Jo Boler's book *Mathematical Mindsets* (Jossey-Bass, 2016) helpful in thinking about how to teach math unconventionally. Paul Lockhart's books (cited in Chapter 9) might inspire you, too.

Summary

In this chapter, we looked at how 3D printing is being used for special needs students, with visually impaired students as a primary focus. The key challenges are model design and teacher access to and ability to use 3D printers. We covered various efforts underway to create standards for models and to encourage more community creation of models that are accessible to all students.

PART IV

Building Lifelong Skills

In Part IV (Chapters 13 and 14) we discuss university and community uses of 3D printing, and how to think about careers in 3D printing in the near and long term. Chapter 13 focuses on research into both applications of 3D printing and technology development for 3D printers. Chapter 14 winds up the book with a discussion of the opportunities and challenges for teaching entrepreneurship, and tries to predict where the manufacturing and other applications of the technology are likely to be in the near and longer term.

CHAPTER 13

University Research Applications

Many aspects of the 3D-printing ecosystem are still very much wide-open research areas. Novel applications and technologies to improve 3D printing will likely be coming thick and fast for a long time. There is a classic cycle of technology adoption called the Gartner Hype Cycle (www.gartner.com/en/research/methodologies/gartner-hype-cycle). In this cycle, when a technology such as low-cost 3D printing comes along, lots of people get excited. There is much over-promising and under-delivering as people rush into what they think might be a multibillion-dollar market. Early adopters buy one because it is cool, not necessarily because they have a use for it. In the case of consumer 3D printing, that peak probably came in 2012 or 2013.

Then there is usually a fall-off and some consolidation. In the case of 3D printers, low-cost producers, many from China, made machines that did not meet unrealistic expectations for ease of use and typically did not provide any tech support that might have eased this. Gartner calls this the *trough of disillusionment*, and many 3D printer companies have indeed gone out of business in the last couple of years. The days are gone when everyone and their brother were putting up 3D printer ideas on Kickstarter.

© Joan Horvath, Rich Cameron 2018
J. Horvath and R. Cameron, *Mastering 3D Printing in the Classroom, Library, and Lab*,
https://doi.org/10.1007/978-1-4842-3501-0_13

Finally, we now seem to be in the more realistic growth period for 3D printing. Users understand that they need to know a bit about the process to get good results, and more sophisticated users are trying to push the boundaries. Some brave souls continue to start 3D printer companies. In this chapter, we look at research areas and advanced applications at the university and corporate research level. In Chapter 14, we speculate about where current students may find future careers in additive manufacturing.

Materials

Chapter 2 covers different materials that are available for 3D printing. As noted there, research in 3D printing is increasingly being driven by materials science research. There are vast arrays of filaments, resins, and powders (for industrial machines) available now, but that does not mean people are no longer doing research.

At the MIT Media Lab, Neri Oxman's group (`www.media.mit.edu/people/neri/projects`) works with many novel materials, including glass. They have developed a process to 3D print large, notably transparent glass pieces.

Other groups at MIT (like the Tangible Media group, `http://tangible.media.mit.edu/projects/`) have also been working with 3D-printing materials that change shape after printing by being heated, for instance, so that they print flat and spring into interesting shapes after being heated, or perhaps inflated.

Printing in concrete is an active research area, too. The Center for Rapid Automated Fabrication Technologies (CRAFT, `www.craft-usc.com`) at USC has been looking into 3D printing with concrete for quite a while. They have developed a technique called *contour crafting*, which lays up a thick, clay-like concrete followed by a blade that smooths away the layer lines. Here, too, developing concrete formulations that can be used this way has been a large part of the research effort. These printers make it possible to create concrete structures without using forms (with a pretty large external gantry). One application that has been proposed for the technology is to build many shelters quickly in the wake of natural disasters. Concrete is a good building material, but it needs reinforcement to make up for its low tensile strength. A number of companies and research groups have been developing ways to create buildings by extruding layers of concrete. They use different methods to add reinforcement to the structures.

These examples, of course, are only a few of the many programs at universities around the world. If you are interested in a particular application or material, searching the peer-reviewed literature will likely yield some results.

Printing Metal

Printing directly in metal is a difficult industrial process and not likely to occur in homes or offices anytime soon. Some companies we talk about in Chapter 2's "Advanced Filaments" section have come out with metal-filled filament that embeds metal in plastic. The mixture is used to print, and then the plastic is baked out. However, if you are moving to an industrial scale, 3D printed metal parts are really coming into their own.

Direct printing of metal usually involves metal powder that is fused by a laser or with some sort of binder (which also needs to be baked out). The challenge is that metal powder is dangerous and difficult to work with, and is even prone to explosions. For that reason, most metal 3D printers operate in an inert gas atmosphere, like argon. The materials handling procedures of powder-based metal 3D printers require significant facilities investments.

With that said, for the right application, metal 3D printing can be a game-changer. One of the bigger producers of direct-metal printers, 3D Systems (`www.3dsystems.com`), has many case studies on its website. Some particularly interesting ones include the following:

- Titanium bone replacements are printed in a fine lattice pattern so that bone will grow into them, a process called *osseointegration.*

- "Lightweighted" aerospace structures are made very strong but light by creating complex parts which have lattice-like structures only where they need to be to carry a load, and open space where they do not.

- Complex parts can be made that combine dozens or even hundreds of previous components, saving assembly time and improving reliability.

More and more alloys are available for 3D printing, too, from steel to aluminum alloys and titanium.

Analyzing Parts

As we have said repeatedly in this book, 3D printers are robots that are really not all that sophisticated, and that may be using materials that have very poorly characterized engineering properties. At this level of sophistication, modeling the stresses experienced by a 3D printed part is challenging, other than by destructively testing an exact replica. This may change over time, but it is one of the factors limiting applications of small printers for tasks that require analyzing stresses on the part in software first.

Industrial printers are in another category entirely. Systems like the large metal printers need sophisticated process control. To complicate matters, if one is designing a part for a critical use, software is needed to model the loads on that part. At the moment, many of the standard engineering software packages that engineers use to design parts cannot handle 3D printed parts well or at all. As discussed in Chapter 9, 3D prints can be stronger in some directions than others, particularly ones that use filament. Printer manufacturer 3D Systems, which has many printers in this market, handles this by selling integrated design and printer control software, with tight specifications for materials.

Generative design software, which creates possible designs for parts based on requirements for them, is evolving as a way to help humans design complex parts optimized for 3D printing—for example, parts with lots of load-bearing latticework. Autodesk is exploring this idea, as described at www.autodesk.com/solutions/generative-design.

Printing Food

3D printed food was a hyped application a few years ago, but this enthusiasm has since been tempered. The reality is that 3D printing is slow (compared to industrial throughput), and managing finicky temperature ranges while making printers food-safe is a challenge. To be food-safe, printers need to have everything that touches food be sterilizable and be made of food-safe materials. To solve these issues, most food printers use some sort of syringe-like device to extrude a paste.

Variety is limited though, because most food printing does not involve the actual programmatic creation or mixing of ingredients, but simply involves extruding these mixtures into predetermined locations (something that is already commonplace in the creation of packaged food). However, printing pieces that can be used to make molds is a promising area of development for customizing the shapes of food products, rather than their compositions.

There are niche printers for chocolate (for example, http://chocedge.com). There are also "3D printers" that make pancakes (www.pancakebot.com), but they are really just drawing in 2D.

Bioprinting

Specialized biological printers (to make human organs, for example) are called *bioprinters,* and we touched on these in Chapter 2. They have similar design constraints to food printers and are also often syringe-based systems. Bioprinters lay down a medium (usually some kind of gel, like alginate) that contains live cells. Cellink (https://cellink.com) has been developing "bioinks" to facilitate other types of structures, and has a multi-head printer that also includes capabilities such as UV sterilization. Different heads can be used to lay down different types of materials that require cooling, say, or heating.

Bioprinters have garnered a lot of press lately, and here the 3D printer part is relatively easy. Learning how to grow tissues that can be accepted by the human body will be the hard part going forward.

Custom Equipment and Prototypes

The next chapter discusses short-run manufacturing and prototyping more generally. In the university environment, 3D printing can be a very cost-effective way to create lab equipment. This is particularly true when no good existing equipment will serve the desired purpose.

We were part of an effort a few years ago to help University of California, Riverside, entomology researchers in Richard Stouthamer's lab design a 3D-printable "emergence trap" for the polyphagous shothole borer (PSHB).

PSHB beetles bore into a tree and deposit a fungus and ultimately eggs for the next generation. The researchers wanted to create a trap that would attach to a tree and catch some of the beetles and the fungus for study, and see how many beetles and their offspring were emerging from the holes they had bored into the trees. 3D printing allowed the scientists to iterate designs as they learned more about what would work, and to have exactly what they wanted.

Note   If you want to read the details of the bug trap case study, it has been published in this scientific journal article: Daniel Berry, Roger D. Selby, Joan C. Horvath, Rich H. Cameron, Diego Porqueras, Richard Stouthamer (February, 2016), "A Modular System of 3D Printed Emergence Traps for Studying the Biology of Shot Hole Borers and Other *Scolytinae." Journal of Economic Entomology*, DOI: 10.1093/jee/tov407.

Another area where 3D printing has made a difference is in experiments that require managing small amounts of fluid, sometimes called *millifluidics,* to distinguish it from the even-smaller *microfluidics.* These applications require custom tiny flow paths to study various fluid properties. For examples, try searching on "millifluidics 3D printing" in the Public Library of Science (PLOS) open-access journals, http://collections.plos.org, for recent work in this space.

Standards

One of the challenges in using 3D printed parts is that filament's mechanical properties can vary widely, even with the colors of a manufacturer's PLA, for instance. For filament-printed parts especially, the part geometry and the relative direction of forces to layer lines matters a lot. Resin print properties can depend both on the resin's mechanical properties and on how well the curing process followed specifications. Parts that require finishing or baking out have uncertainties introduced in those steps.

Various groups have been wrestling with testing common 3D-printing materials for qualities like strength and chemical interactions, but it is challenging. Some groups working in this space include the following:

- Joshua Pearce's group at Michigan Technological University has been publishing about their attempts to get realistic numbers for some of these key mechanical and chemical properties. Many papers are linked in their Appropedia wiki at `www.appropedia.org/Pearce_publications_in_materials_science_and_engineering`.

- The American National Standards Institute (ANSI) and various collaborators are working on a standard: `www.ansi.org/standards_activities/standards_boards_panels/amsc/`.

- ASTM has standards, including those for specific metals, at `www.astm.org/Standards/additive-manufacturing-technology-standards.html`.

There is a lot of work to do here, and thorough characterizations of materials and geometries will be a research effort for some time to come.

Summary

Researchers at the university level have many options to improve the 3D-printing process: by creating new materials, finding novel ways to use existing ones, and finding new applications. There is still much work to be done to make 3D printing easier to use, and to make the physical and chemical properties of 3D prints more consistent and reliable for demanding applications. Meanwhile, scientists can take advantage of the technology to create custom equipment that can let them explore frontiers more cheaply and creatively than might have seemed possible before the ubiquity of low-cost printers.

CHAPTER 14

Community and Careers

We are often asked what types of 3D printing–related jobs will be available in the future. Since it is pretty challenging to predict where the industry will go in the next couple of years, much less in a decade or two, any attempt to answer should be taken with a large grain of salt. Any 3D printer that a student uses now will have very little resemblance to an industrial printer used for metal parts. However, the skill of being able to envision something, create a computer model of it, and then transform that into a physical object will always be a valuable one.

Note We have found that many people coming into this space are comfortable with either the computer design part of it or the physical fabrication. People comfortable with both are less common. This is one reason that we encourage having students run their own print jobs, once they are old enough. There is no substitute for actual experience making things—it is like the difference between watching someone play a sport and trying it yourself.

What, then, is the best way to approach preparing students for the economy they are likely to work in? First, training in technical subjects is always a basic requirement, and figuring out how to make a physical

J. Horvath and R. Cameron, *Mastering 3D Printing in the Classroom, Library, and Lab*, https://doi.org/10.1007/978-1-4842-3501-0_14

part that will hold together and do whatever it is supposed to do is a great way to teach many engineering basics. The physicality of the product (instead of something on a screen) can also help students think about making a product useful and attractive (or even fun) instead of just creating something that can support a load. For students thinking about a career in the arts, digital manufacturing can increase their reach in a new medium. Finally, physically creating something often requires teamwork to bring together the many strengths needed for successful maker projects. Sometimes student team projects can seem contrived, but to make something, teams will often form organically, because so many skills are typically needed.

Student Entrepreneurship

If students have reasonably free access to a makerspace, sooner or later some of them will invent a product that their peers want. Whether it is a toy or something with the school logo for sporting events, what happens if you suddenly have an inventor on your hands with a market? It is best to think about this ahead of time and, if you are at a public school, to find out if your district has policies about students using equipment for profit. Some things to consider:

- Who owns the designs invented at school, whether for a school project or something else?

- Can students use school materials to make ten of something for their friends, if they do not charge for it?

- Can students bring materials in and use school printers (or other equipment) to make things they then subsequently sell?

- Are there tax and liability implications for the student and/or the school?

We cover some of the practicalities of running a 3D printer and its facilities needs in Chapter 5. Take a look particularly at the "Where Should We Put It?" Section.

Tip   Schools need to decide whether they can encourage and support entrepreneurship, and how far they can go in that support. Universities have wrestled with this for a long time (the department that handles these things is usually called the "technology transfer" or "licensing" group), and if you want to encourage this in a big way, you might talk to a local university tech transfer office that knows your school system and community.

Students might learn about these technologies at school and want to start a business at home. If the student's parents are able to provide a printer and supplies and give them access to legal and tax advice, then there are a variety of marketplaces (like www.tindie.com and www.etsy.com) that might serve as outlets. A crowdfunding site (like Kickstarter, www.kickstarter.com) can be an option for more ambitious ideas.

Caution   It is important to stay realistic. Making, marketing, and selling a product are not easy, and standard business advice of keeping overhead low applies. If a product is successful, keeping up with demand and doing the printing, packing, and shipping can become substantial endeavors. Many Kickstarter campaigns fail to deliver after being funded because their creator did not properly budget for their time and all the other expenses, beyond raw materials, that would be required to deliver on their promises. And of course, there is always the risk that the idea will be copied by someone bigger if it is very successful.

This all sounds very exciting and like the classic company-in-a-garage dream. What happens, though, if the student's parents cannot afford to capitalize equipment or pay for a bit of legal or accounting advice? Age limits on various business activities such as selling on a site can be an issue, too, if there is no parent support of the young entrepreneur, and this is likely to vary in different states and countries, too. Such students may be creating jobs for themselves in an area where jobs are few and far between, but they will need some help to get going.

There are charter schools like Prime School in Los Angeles (www.primeschool.org, planned for launch in 2019) that have entrepreneurship in high-poverty areas as a core focus. The availability of both maker tools and Internet selling platforms has dramatically lowered the cost of entry for product entrepreneurs and 3D-printing service providers. Schools are starting to look to leverage these tools for student and community benefit. We hope that the business and maker community will help these entrepreneurs use maker tech and Internet tools to create enterprises where there were none before.

Note   The business of using consumer 3D printers to print jobs for the general public has become rather low-margin, at least in California where competition has driven down prices. Sites like www.3dhubs.com let printer owners bid on printing jobs that people post, and anecdotally bids seem to be quite reasonable now for straightforward prints in PLA. This is good for the consumer wanting something printed and for someone doing it in their garage for extra money. It is a low-margin business, particularly because print files submitted often need some substantial rework before printing. We suspect that many of these are teens doing print jobs as an alternative to mowing lawns, and we have dubbed this phenomenon the "digital lemonade stand." Professional service bureaus seem to be migrating more to specialized prints that require expensive equipment, or to combining scanning, 3D design, and printing services under one roof.

Public Library Makerspaces

Numerous public libraries have been putting in makerspaces for their communities. In many cases, the presumption is that the majority of users will be children and teens, and the "teen librarian" often seems to be the one who winds up managing it. Obviously, adults wanting to retrain themselves can be beneficiaries, too (learning either the computer or hands-on skills or both). For some reason, 3D printers are often seen by libraries as a kid thing, which we think is too limiting.

The issues we mention earlier in the chapter for schools also apply to a library. The situation is a little different, though, in that a library is intended to be a public resource. The question becomes how much any one person can monopolize the resource, and how the makerspace can sustain itself if it does not have long-term funding.

Libraries have to decide whether they want to be at-cost or no-cost 3D printing and perhaps laser-cutting service bureaus for the community, for example, and whether that puts them in competition with for-profit local businesses. Setting priorities for printer access and policies about what can be printed are important, too. Finally, there will need to be a process to be sure that the right materials are used with any maker machinery. See Chapter 1 for laser cutter concerns and Chapter 2 for 3D-printer materials compatibility.

Some libraries are older civic buildings, and finding a place that has power, that can keep the equipment secure, and that has adequate ventilation can be a challenge. Often there is money donated to buy equipment, but not to renovate any space or train staff. This can require a bit of creativity.

Caution   Unfortunately, sometimes schools or libraries have equipment donated that does not work or that is more expensive to run than a newer machine might be. If you are in charge of a nonprofit makerspace, ask gentle questions if your donors are giving you used equipment. Otherwise, a lot of staff time and frustration can be spent trying to get something broken to work when you assume it is you or your staff, not the equipment, that is the problem. Or you might have trouble finding proprietary materials if the machine is no longer made.

Libraries can play a key role in letting the public know what it is possible to do with low-cost 3D printers and other maker technologies, such as small electronics. Figure 14-1 shows Joan running a demonstration table with a lot of 3D prints and some fashion tech electronics demonstration. This event was at the Pasadena Public Library's official grand opening of its makerspace. Often people need some inspiration to understand the possibilities, so if you are a librarian opening a space, reach out to local groups to display what they are doing to inspire everyone. Competitions and displays of finished projects are a great way to invite community involvement, too.

Projects that serve the community, ranging from designing citizen science equipment to helping community theater, can be developed over time.

Figure 14-1. *Joan demonstrating various types of maker tech at a library*

Digital Fabrication Career Opportunities

What a student learns on a small consumer 3D printer may not transfer directly to more sophisticated industrial machines, but the intuition helps. Today, 3D printing is being used in a few applications where it adds a lot of value. In this section, we list some typical applications, both to survey the state of the art and perhaps suggest areas for student projects or research to prepare for entering the industry someday. As experience and appropriate automation grow, this list is likely to grow as well.

Prototyping

3D printing has been used for prototyping for decades, and that remains a major application. Now that there are many materials that can be 3D printed (Chapter 2), it is a lot easier to create a model that mimics the form and fit of a product to see how it feels or works with other parts.

Architects and others who need to visualize and discuss complex structures with clients can also benefit from 3D printed models, or incorporate 3D printed pieces into more traditional models of structures. Figure 14-2, for example, is a typical industrial part, prototyped by 3D printer manufacturer MAKEiT, Inc. (http://makeit-3d.com/) in carbon fiber-infused filament.

Figure 14-2. *Carbon fiber filament part (part courtesy of MAKEiT, Inc.)*

Bridge Manufacturing

Manufacturers often use "just in time" methods to keep parts in stock. This means that they do not keep a lot of inventory on hand, and sometimes a whole line will have to stop to wait for a part. To get through that and keep the line running, manufacturers turn to *bridge* parts, made in some other way than the regular process.

Since there are so many materials now, the bridge parts can often be 3D printed in the same material as the production part. This means, in turn, that the finished product can be shipped with the bridge part, and it might not need to be replaced (if quality control requirements allow use of a 3D printed part).

Short-Run Manufacturing

The next step up from bridge manufacturing is to plan to 3D print your manufacturing run of parts in the first place. Some of the early adopters of this were, not surprisingly, the 3D-printer manufacturers themselves. Figure 14-3 shows 3D-printer manufacturer MAKEiT's in-house product facility doing a short run of custom speaker housings designed by Russell Singer, one of the staff.

Printing the same parts over and over can be pretty efficient, since it is worth it to really optimize the printer settings and then just launch the same job over and over. However, 3D printing can be slow for some applications, and the issues with being able to model a part's mechanical properties to a high enough fidelity might be problematic in some applications.

Tip   Because it is possible to 3D print shapes that would be difficult or impossible to manufacture by more conventional methods, you may be able to print what would otherwise be a complicated assembly in far fewer pieces, saving worker time.

Figure 14-3. *Short-run manufacturing (courtesy of Russell Singer/ MAKEiT, Inc.)*

Mass Customization

It is not a big step to go from manufacturing a small number of identical parts one at a time to asking whether one can make a standard part customizable instead. A CAD model might have just a few parameters that can be tweaked depending on what the user needs, or the individual product might be made from a scan.

Dentists have been early adopters of this approach, since almost all of what they do is custom to every patient. Most of the current dental applications use resin printers to create devices that do not go in the mouth themselves but are used as molds for casting, vacuum forming, or other technologies.

Moving to metal printing, orthopedists have been printing artificial hips and other implants. They are printed, typically in a titanium alloy, with surface texture that allows the bone to grow into and fuse with the implant, a process known as *osseointegration* (Figure 14-4). Moving beyond orthopedics, mentioned in the preceding chapter, printing entire organs is an evolving field that has great promise for many medical conditions.

Figure 14-4. *3D Systems ProX® DMP 320 printers and K2M's advanced methodologies called Lamellar 3D Titanium Technology™ enable K2M to produce structures in its CASCADIA™ Interbody Systems that provide both porosity and surface roughness to allow for bone growth (image courtesy of 3D Systems)*

3D printed fashion (notably shoes and high fashion at this point) is in its early days, and is mostly used for prototyping or high-visibility pieces for celebrity clients or athletes. A 3D printed dress created by designer Michael Schmidt (www.michaelschmidtstudios.com) and technologist Francisco Bitoni for Dita von Teese was an early (rather revealing) printed lacework-like dress.

Designers Nervous System (https://n-e-r-v-o-u-s.com) created the "Kinematic Dress," which, like chain armor, folds up for printing (on an SLS machine) and then flows nicely for the wearer. Other novel, 3D printed high fashion has been created by Anouk Wipprecht (www.anoukwipprecht.nl)—famously, her "Spider Dress," which attacked anyone who got too close with animatronic legs. In the next section, we will look at creating jewelry by using 3D prints as a mold.

Note   We can think of these applications as "hardware as a service," in which a digital file can be tweaked and manufactured anyplace an appropriate fabrication machine exists.

Industrial Moldmaking

A somewhat more conventional application of 3D prints is as forms or molds. Either a 3D printed part can be used as the positive to create a negative mold, or a negative mold can be created with 3D printing directly. PLA or specially formulated resins are commonly used to make jewelry from 3D prints via *investment* (or *lost-wax*) casting. In this process, a positive mold called a *pattern* is created, and then ceramic is laid up around it. The ceramic is fired, and the wax, resin, or PLA melts out. Then metal is poured in to make the jewelry piece. Finally, the ceramic mold must be broken to remove the metal piece, so each one can only be used once.

Beginning the process again would traditionally involve carving a new wax pattern that will inevitably end up slightly different from the first. However, a 3D printed pattern can be reproduced precisely just by running the print again. You can change some numbers in the CAD file if it was not quite right and try again, or customize the design for another client.

There is some early work by Formlabs to create a resin that can be used for injection molds. As this evolves, it might enable lower-volume injection molding runs, since this drastically lowers tooling costs and turnaround time.

Tip   Trying out 3D printed tooling or other in-house parts is a good way to test out 3D printing with something that is not going to a customer.

Direct Metal 3D Printing

At the moment, printing directly in metal is a challenging process, requiring sophisticated facilities management. However, ways around that are being explored, as we mention in Chapter 2. Metal 3D printing has incredible promise for making complex, multi-element parts that will be light and very reliable.

We expect that technology development for and applications of the various types of metal printing will continue to grow rapidly. Manufacturer 3D Systems (`www.3dsystems.com`) has many good case studies on its website.

Summary

In this chapter, we started out by framing the issues for student entrepreneurship in school or in enterprises that might be spun out from a school project. Next, we thought about libraries and how these community centers might foster local entrepreneurs. Finally, we surveyed the state of the practice of the use of 3D printing in industry to provide some ideas to guide preparation of the future stars of the design studio and factory floor.

APPENDIX

Links and Resources

Front Matter

Nonscriptum LLC: www.nonscriptum.com

Chapter 1

Reprap Project on Wikipedia: http://en.wikipedia.org/wiki/RepRap_Project
 Reprap Family Tree: http://reprap.org/wiki/RepRap_Family_Tree
 Kickstarter: www.kickstarter.com
 Arc Gimbal on Youmagine: www.youmagine.com/designs/arc-gimbal

Chapter 2

Buildtak: www.buildtak.com
 Markforged: www.markforged.com
 Formlabs: www.formlabs.com
 Pancakebot: www.pancakebot.com
 Organovo: www.organovo.com
 SE3D: www.se3d.com

© Joan Horvath, Rich Cameron 2018
J. Horvath and R. Cameron, *Mastering 3D Printing in the Classroom, Library, and Lab*,
https://doi.org/10.1007/978-1-4842-3501-0

Chapter 3

3MF file format: https://3mf.io/what-is-3mf/
    Thingiverse: www.thingiverse.com
    Youmagine: www.youmagine.com
    Instructables: www.instructables.com
    Pinshape: www.pinshape.com
    Github: www.github.org
    Creative Commons: www.creativecommons.org
    Reprap Project: www.reprap.org
    Slic3r: www.slic3r.org
    MatterControl: www.mattercontrol.com
    Cura: https://ultimaker.com/en/products/ultimaker-cura-software
    Meshlab: www.meshlab.net
    Netfabb: www.autodesk.com/products/netfabb/overview
    G-code reference: http://reprap.org/wiki/G-code
    Octoprint: www.octoprint.org
    Creation Workshop: https://datatree3d.com/software/
    NanoDLP: www.nanodlp.com/download/

Chapter 4

3D Hubs: www.3dhubs.com
    MakeXYZ: www.makexyz.com

Chapter 5

Tinkercad: www.tinkercad.com
    Blick Art Materials: www.dickblick.com

Chapter 6

Protein Databank: www.rcsb.org/pdb/

Chimera: www.cgl.ucsf.edu/chimera/

Visual Molecular Dynamics: www.ks.uiuc.edu/Research/vmd/

National Institutes of Health repository of medicine-related models: https://3dprint.nih.gov

The Smithsonian 3D scan repository: https://3d.si.edu

OpenSCAD: www.openscad.org

Tinkercad Circuits: www.tinkercad.com/circuits

Morphi: www.morphiapp.com

Inkscape: https://inkscape.org

Onshape: www.onshape.com

Fusion360: www.autodesk.com/products/fusion-360

Solidworks: www.solidworks.com

Sketchup: www.sketchup.com

Mathematica: www.wolfram.com/mathematica/

Zbrush: www.zbrush.com

Blender: www.blender.org

Maya: www.autodesk.com/products/maya

Chapter 7

(n/a)

Chapter 8

3D Printing on Fabric: www.thingiverse.com/ShoreyDesigns/designs

XTC-3D: www.smooth-on.com/product-line/xtc-3d/

Maker Faire: www.makerfaire.com

Chapter 9

Appropedia: www.appropedia.org/Open-source_Lab

FIRST Robotics: www.firstinspires.org

Tensile Strength of Commercial Polymer Materials for Fused Filament Fabrication 3-D Printing on Appropedia: www.appropedia.org/Tensile_Strength_of_Commercial_Polymer_Materials_for_Fused_Filament_Fabrication_3-D_Printing

Proto-Pasta Conductive PLA: www.proto-pasta.com/collections/exotic-composite-pla/products/conductive-pla

Zooniverse: www.zooniverse.org

Hacker Calculus: https://hackaday.io/project/20621-hacker-calculus

Chapter 10

Terrain2STL: http://jthatch.com/Terrain2STL/

Moon2STL: http://jthatch.com/Moon2STL/

Meshmixer: www.meshmixer.com

3D Vermont: http://3dvermont.org

Chapter 11

Lucie deLaBruere's journal: http://createmakelearn.blogspot.com

John Umekubo's website: https://johnumekubo.com

Chapter 12

The Neil Squire Society: www.neilsquire.ca

DIAGRAM Center: http://diagramcenter.org/3d-printing.html

Constant-Volume Models: www.youmagine.com/designs/fixed-volume-objects

Braille script in OpenSCAD: `https://github.com/whosawhatsis/braille-openscad`

3D Printed Education Models Google Group: `https://groups.google.com/forum/#!forum/3dp_edu_models`

Chapter 13

Gartner Hype Cycle: `www.gartner.com/en/research/methodologies/gartner-hype-cycle`

Neri Oxman's group at the MIT Media Lab: `www.media.mit.edu/people/neri/projects`

MIT Tangible Media group: `http://tangible.media.mit.edu/projects/`

Center for Rapid Automated Fabrication Technologies: `www.craft-usc.com`

3D Systems: `www.3dsystems.com`

Autodesk's generative design software: `www.autodesk.com/solutions/generative-design`

Chocolate 3D printer: `http://chocedge.com`

Cellink: `https://cellink.com`

Public Library of Science (PLOS) open-access journals: `http://collections.plos.org`

Pearce publications in materials science and engineering on Appropedia: `www.appropedia.org/Pearce_publications_in_materials_science_and_engineering`

America Makes & ANSI Additive Manufacturing Standardization Collaborative: `www.ansi.org/standards_activities/standards_boards_panels/amsc/`

ATSM Additive Manufacturing Technology Standards: `www.astm.org/Standards/additive-manufacturing-technology-standards.html`

Chapter 14

Tindie: www.tindie.com

Etsy: www.etsy.com

Prime School: www.primeschool.org

MAKEiT, Inc.: http://makeit-3d.com

Michael Schmidt: www.michaelschmidtstudios.com

Nervous System: https://n-e-r-v-o-u-s.com

Anouk Wipprecht: www.anoukwipprecht.nl

Media Sites Focusing on 3D Printing

This last group of sites are media organizations that focus on 3D printing and/or the maker movement. Many blogs and informal sites as well as major news organizations cover 3D printing—a web search on the topic of interest will reveal a mix of traditional and upstart media coverage.

3D Printing Industry (industry website): http://3dprintingindustry.com

Make magazine (website and physical magazine): www.makezine.com

Hackaday (website): www.hackaday.com

3Ders (websites and community forums): www.3ders.org

Books

We have a fairly eclectic set of books that we have found useful, some of which we have explicitly mentioned in the text, and others of which are classic design texts or just books that made us think. You may find some of them useful as you try to think about how to effectively incorporate maker ideas into teaching and learning:

Armstrong, T. (2012) *Neurodiversity in the Classroom*. Alexandria, VA: ASCD Press

Boeler, J. (2016) *Mathematical Mindsets*. San Francisco: Jossey-Bass

Horvath, J. and Cameron, R. (2016) *3D Printed Science Projects*. New York: Apress

Horvath, J. and Cameron, R. (2017) *3D Printed Science Projects, Volume 2*. New York: Apress

Lockhart, P. (2009) *A Mathematician's Lament*. New York: Bellevue Literary Press

Norman, D.A. (1988) *The Design of Everyday Things*. Basic Books

Resnick, M. (2017) *Lifelong Kindergarten*. The MIT Press

Petroski, H. (1992) *To Engineer Is Human*. Vintage Books

Index

A

Additive manufacturing, 4, 6
Allan, Jim, 264, 268
American National Standards
    Institute (ANSI), 280
Appropedia, 280

B

Batschelet, Rodney, 211–213, 256
Benetech, 264, 268
Bioprinting, 49, 278
Bitoni, Francisco, 291
Boler, Jo, 269
Bowyer, Adrian, 7
Bridge, 30
Butterfrog, 211

C

Calipers, 32
Career opportunities, 3D printing
    bridge manufacturing, 288–289
    mass customization, 290–291
    prototyping, 288
    short-run manufacturing,
      289–290

Casting from 3D print
    investment casting, 218–221
    lost-wax casting, 218
    vs. printing in metal, 222
    sand casting, 215, 217–218
Casting services (metal), 222
Cellink, 278
Center for Rapid Automated
    Fabrication Technologies
    (CRAFT), 274
Cheverie, Michael, 268
Citizen science, 240
Clogged nozzle solutions, 122, 139
    cold pull technique, 140–143
    hard clogs, 144–145
Cold pull technique, 136, 141–143
Computer-aided design (CAD),
    52–53, 56–57, 59, 72, 84
Computer numerically controlled
    machine (CNC), 11, 13
Conductive 3D prints, 239–240
Constant-volume models
    lack of Braille labels, 265
    storytelling aspects, 265
Contour crafting, 274
Cooling tower, 201
Creative commons licenses, 55

© Joan Horvath, Rich Cameron 2018
J. Horvath and R. Cameron, *Mastering 3D Printing in the Classroom, Library, and Lab*,
https://doi.org/10.1007/978-1-4842-3501-0

Printed in the United States
By Bookmasters